# HIGH-FLAVOR, LOW-FAT PASTA

Steven Raichlen's

———

# HIGH-FLAVOR, LOW-FAT PASTA

*Photography by Greg Schneider*

VIKING

VIKING
Published by the Penguin Group
Penguin Books USA Inc., 375 Hudson Street,
New York, New York 10014, U.S.A.
Penguin Books Ltd, 27 Wrights Lane,
London W8 5TZ, England
Penguin Books Australia Ltd, Ringwood,
Victoria, Australia
Penguin Books Canada Ltd, 10 Alcorn Avenue,
Toronto, Ontario, Canada M4V 3B2
Penguin Books (N.Z.) Ltd, 182–190 Wairau Road,
Auckland 10, New Zealand

Penguin Books Ltd, Registered Offices:
Harmondsworth, Middlesex, England

First published in 1996 by Viking Penguin,
a division of Penguin Books USA Inc.

10 9 8 7 6 5 4 3 2

Library of Congress Cataloging in Publication Data
Raichlen, Steven.
   High-flavor, low-fat pasta / Steven Raichlen ; photography by Greg Schneider.
      p.   cm.
   Includes index.
   ISBN 0-670-86581-8
   1. Cookery (Pasta).   2. Low-fat diet—Recipes.   I. Title.
TX809.M17R35     1996
641.8´22—dc20     95–24620

This book is printed on acid-free paper.

Printed in the United States of America
Set in Goudy Old Style
Designed by Katy Riegel

*To my parents, Sonny and Cecille Raichlen,*
*in honor of their twenty-fifth anniversary.*
*Congratulations!*

# ACKNOWLEDGMENTS

It gives me great pleasure to acknowledge the people who helped make this book possible.

First, son Jake, who makes his debut as a recipe tester and chef.

Next, Elida Proenza, Bruce Frankel, and Kevin Pierce, who also brought sound judgment and keen taste buds to the testing process.

Greg Schneider animates my recipes with his boundless energy and stunning photographs. He was assisted by the ever cheerful Michael Donnelly. Debbie Chelotis provided logistical support in the office, and Karen Brasel once again supplied nutritional analyses.

Dawn Drzal at Viking Penguin graced the manuscript with her expert editing, as did Theodora Rosenbaum. I'd like to thank all my friends at Viking for their enthusiasm and support, including Barbara Grossman, Cathy Hemming, Norm Sheinman, Paul Slovak, Tamar Mendelson, Alix MacGowan, and Katy Riegel.

I would like to thank the tourism boards of Japan, Singapore, and Thailand, who helped facilitate my research of Asian noodles.

Above all, I want to thank my wife, Barbara, whose savvy, support, and love made this—and all my books—possible. You're the best!

## PHOTO CREDITS

The author would like to thank the following individuals and businesses for help with styling and props: Arianna's Cookshop, South Miami, Florida; Delores "D.J." Sticht and Burdines, Miami, Florida; Yvette Kalinowski and Iberia Tiles, Miami, Florida; Modernage Furniture, Miami, Florida; Manuel Revuelta, artist (sculpted plates), Miami, Florida.

# CONTENTS

# INTRODUCTION

In the Tower of Babel of the world's cuisines, one dish is universally understood: pasta. This culinary common denominator is savored around the world—from Pisa to Peking to Providence. Pasta and noodle dishes turn up at fancy restaurants, homey trattorias, and humble Third World market stalls, enjoyed with gusto by rich and poor alike. Satisfying and sustaining, healthy and nutritious, pasta is surely one of the most perfect dishes ever devised.

American interest in pasta and noodle dishes has exploded in the last decade—fueled in part by the proliferation of Italian and Asian restaurants and in part by our growing health consciousness. You don't need a degree in nutrition to know that health experts of all stripes recommend a diet based on grains, with sparing use of meats and dairy products. Grains are literally the foundation of the Department of Agriculture's Food Guide Pyramid. And a great deal of the world's wheat and other grains wind up in some sort of noodle.

Pasta is also the ideal dish for the time-starved 1990s, offering nutritious meals with a minimum of preparation time. It's the perfect food to prepare when you come home tired from work. To this, add the incredible diversity of noodles, from Italian pasta to Moroccan couscous to Chinese rice noodles and bean threads, and you'll understand why America's passion for pasta is growing all the time.

Not all pasta dishes are automatically healthy, however. Just think of a cream-drenched alfredo or a butter-laden linguini with clam sauce. Pesto, that summery sauce of the Italian Riviera, contains high levels of nuts, cheese, and olive oil.

When I set out to write this book, I was faced with a special challenge. How do you create quick, easy, great-tasting pasta dishes using low levels of fat?

The answer is simple: high-flavor, low-fat cooking. Let intense flavorings—not fat—make your food taste delicious. In the old days, we enriched pasta dishes with generous doses of butter, cream, egg yolks, and olive oil. This is especially true for cooks, like myself, who learned to cook in the 1970s and 1980s, when most of our inspiration came from Italy and France.

These days, health-conscious cooks prefer the richness of fresh herbs, tongue-tingling chilies, and tangy condiments from Asia and the Caribbean to animal fats. It's not without reason that the 1990s has been called the "flavor decade." The modern cook has at his or her disposal an unprecedented selection of seasonings from around the world. We live in a global village, with a global economy and world music. The same is true for our cooking. These days, you have only to visit a local supermarket to find flavorings and ingredients that just a decade ago would have seemed downright exotic.

This emphasis on flavor over fat enables you to create great-tasting dishes that are good for you. We're talking about a different sort of richness here. Not the unctuous, artery-clogging richness of yesteryear's butter and cream sauces. But a clean, bold, big-flavored richness that lights up your mouth like a Fourth of July sky.

As in all my high-flavor, low-fat books—and in accordance with modern health precepts—I've tried to keep the percentage of calories derived from fat in my recipes to 30 percent or less. That translates to seven to ten grams of fat per serving in most cases, sometimes less. But please note that my cooking is low fat, not no fat. Call

me a pragmatist or a closet hedonist. I'm not looking to make fat-free meals that taste more like medicine than like food. I'd rather use a little fat to create dishes you'll want to serve again and again.

## ABOUT THE RECIPES IN THIS BOOK

This book contains forty pasta and noodle recipes gathered literally from all over the world. Some are low-fat remakes of old favorites such as fettuccine primavera and spaghetti with clam sauce. Others were inspired by my travels: lunch at a Tokyo noodle shop or dinner at a Tuscan trattoria. The recipes cover all phases of a meal: soups, salads, stir-fries, casseroles, and, of course, pasta entrees with sauce. There's even a sweet noodle pudding you can enjoy for breakfast or dessert.

The first thing you may notice if you're a newcomer to my style of cooking is a lavish (some might say profligate) use of seasonings. I like dishes with big, complex flavors. My recipes may call for more ingredients than you're used to. This doesn't necessarily mean that they're more complicated or time-consuming. It just means they have more taste.

Nonetheless, recognizing that some people may not like food seasoned quite as highly as I do, I often offer a range for strong-flavored ingredients, such as chili peppers or fish sauce. The timid of taste may wish to start with the minimum quantities. Optional ingredients, like anchovies and chili paste, can certainly be omitted if they make you nervous.

I've tried to offer a similar freedom of choice in pasta types, garnishes, and meats. The great thing about pasta cookery is that it is something you can do at the last minute. If you're anything like me, you may not decide what to cook until you get home from work and look through the refrigerator. I'd hate to think of someone not trying one of my recipes because they lack a particular ingredient. Some of my best creations have resulted from spur-of-the-moment substitutions.

Feel free to use snap peas or broccoli florets in a recipe that calls for asparagus or green beans. By all means, substitute chicken, shrimp, tofu, or extra vegetables in a recipe that calls for beef. My recipes are intended as a framework, a road map—not as a slavish text to be followed to the letter. Use these recipes as a springboard for your own creativity and you'll have captured the spirit of my cooking.

The same holds true for pasta. There's more to the diversity of pasta shapes than mere whimsy on the part of the noodle-maker (although this is certainly a factor). Over the centuries, certain types of pasta have come to be associated with certain dishes: long, slender noodles for wet and creamy sauces; coiled or twisted pasta for chunky sauces (the vegetable pieces lodge in the coils);

small pasta tubes for salads and casseroles; shells and sheets of pasta for stuffing.

Within this broad framework, as far as I'm concerned, anything goes. Linguini, perciatelli, or capellini will work perfectly well in a recipe calling for spaghetti. Pasta salads can be made just as easily with penne, ziti, or *cavatappi* (corkscrews) as with macaroni or shells. Again, let creativity and what you have on hand be your guide.

## BUYING AND COOKING PASTA AND NOODLES

I don't know if anyone has ever attempted to catalogue all the different types of pasta and noodles in the world. I'm sure the roster would run in the thousands. Soft, silky egg pasta from Bologna. Slippery rice sticks from Chiang Mai. Moroccan couscous no bigger than grains of sand. Italy alone makes hundreds of whimsically shaped dried pastas, ranging from *lumache* (snails) and *orecchiette* (little ears) to *farfalle* (butterflies) and *ruote di carro* (cartwheels).

For the purposes of this book, there are two main catagories of pasta: fresh and dried. The first—traditionally associated with northern Italy—is made with regular or semolina flour and eggs. The dough is rolled into thin sheets, which are cut into noodles of varying widths. Instructions on making egg pasta from scratch are beyond the scope of this book. (There are many excellent works on the subject, including Giuliano Hazan's *The Classic Pasta Cookbook*, Dorling Kindersley, 1993, and Giuliano Bugialli's *Bugialli on Pasta*, Simon & Schuster, 1988.) Chinese wonton wrappers can be used in place of homemade egg pasta for making ravioli and other stuffed pastas. (See the Shrimp Ravioli on page 35.)

In the last five years, fresh egg pasta has become widely available at gourmet shops and supermarkets. Or you can invest in a pasta machine, like the Pasta Maker by Cuisinart, which kneads and shapes the dough for you at the push of a button. One thing the low-fat cook should keep in mind about fresh pasta is that one of its main ingredients is eggs. For this reason, I make it a splurge pasta rather than daily fare.

The other type of pasta is dried. Traditionally associated with southern Italy, dried pasta is made from hard durum wheat and water. The dough is extruded through an industrial press into strands, shells, squiggles, tubes, and a host of other shapes. Unlike fresh pasta, dried pasta contains no fat or cholesterol. Most of the recipes in this book call for dried pasta. (Feel free to substitute dried pasta in the few recipes calling for fresh pasta.) The various pasta shapes and sizes are discussed in full in the Pasta Primer on pages 71–72.

The Italians have a wonderful expression for properly cooked pasta: al dente, literally "to the tooth." This means that, while the pasta should be completely cooked, it should still have a little chew to it. It definitely shouldn't be soft. The best way to test for doneness is to taste the pasta. Rinse a noodle with cold water before testing, so you don't burn your tongue.

When cooking pasta, it's essential to use plenty of water—at least four quarts for eight ounces of dried pasta or one pound fresh pasta. The more water you use, the less gummy or starchy the cooked pasta will be. The water should be rapidly boiling when you add the pasta and kept at a rolling boil during the cooking. Some cooks like to add salt or a little oil to the water: the former for extra flavor, the latter to keep the noodles from sticking together. I generally omit these ingredients in the following recipes, but you can certainly add them if you wish.

One thing I often do is rinse the pasta under water after cooking. This washes off any excess starch and keeps the pasta from overcooking or clumping together. Rinsing with cold water is especially important for pasta salads; you want the noodle to keep a little of its chew.

The last step is to simmer the cooked pasta in the sauce for a few minutes before serving to impregnate it with sauce.

When serving fresh pasta, figure on 5 to 6 ounces per person. When serving dried pasta, figure on 2 to 3 ounces per person. One pound of spaghetti, linguini, or other long, slender pasta will serve 6 to 8. Shell- and tube-shaped pastas generally double in bulk when cooked. Most of my recipes yield 4 servings, but you can quarter or halve the recipe to serve 1 or 2.

## ABOUT ASIAN NOODLES

Just when you thought you'd mastered the fine points of Italian pasta, a new wave of noodles is upon us. Once the province of ethnic markets, rice sticks, bean threads, and other Asian noodles have begun to turn up en masse at our local supermarkets and restaurants.

The noodles of the Orient are incredibly diverse. Unlike in the West, where pasta is made chiefly from wheat flour, Asians prepare noodles from buckwheat and rice flour, mung bean and potato starch, and even from sweet potatoes and yams. Asian noodles can be as thin as thread or as thick as broomsticks, square, round, rectangular, flat, string-shaped or rounded like teardrops. The various types are discussed in the Pasta Primer on pages 72–73.

Fresh wheat and rice noodles should be fluffed with your fingers before cooking. Dried noodles, particularly rice noodles and bean threads, tend to shatter when handled: Open the packages and break apart clumps in a large bowl or paper bag to keep noodle pieces from flying all over your kitchen.

Dry rice noodles and bean threads should be soaked in warm water for twenty minutes or until soft and pliable. Cook them briefly (one to two minutes); prolonged boiling will reduce them to a gelatinous mass.

Like Western pasta, Oriental noodles should be cooked in lots of boiling water, at least four quarts for one pound of noodles. Asians tend to eat their noodles slightly softer than Italian al dente.

## A WORD ABOUT INGREDIENTS AND COOKING TECHNIQUES

Most of the recipes in this book can be prepared with ingredients from your local supermarket. Exotic ingredients are discussed in the notes at the end of the particular recipes. Here are my thoughts on some specific ingredients used widely in *High-Flavor, Low-Fat Pasta.*

TOMATOES: A soft, juicy, vine-ripened tomato is one of life's gustatory glories. Look for such specimens at farm stands when tomatoes are in season in your area. Let less-than-ripe tomatoes ripen at room temperature on a windowsill or in a paper bag. *Never* refrigerate a tomato. (The cold prevents immature tomatoes from ripening and makes ripe ones taste mealy.) If you can't find good fresh tomatoes, you may be better off using a good canned imported brand.

When you can find ripe tomatoes, it's worth the effort to peel and seed them before adding them to pasta dishes. Why? Cooked tomato skins can form red filaments that get caught in your teeth when you eat them. And some people feel that the watery pulp inside a tomato dilutes the flavor of the sauce.

To peel a tomato, use the tip of a paring knife to cut out the stem end. Score a shallow X in the rounded end. Plunge the tomato in rapidly boiling water for 15 to 60 seconds. (The riper the tomato, the shorter the cooking time.) Let the tomato cool on a plate until you can comfortably handle it, then pull off the skin with your fingers. It should slip off in broad strips.

To seed a tomato, cut it in half widthwise and squeeze each half in the palm of your hand, cut side down, to wring out the seeds and liquid. Work over a bowl and strainer. Push the pulp through the strainer with the back of a spoon. Reserve the tomato liquid that collects in the bowl for sauces, soups, or even drinking. One large tomato (9 to 10 ounces) yields ¾ to 1 cup peeled, seeded, chopped flesh.

GARLIC: Use fresh garlic for these recipes. Lots! For ease in chopping, throw a dozen or so peeled cloves in a food processor and process until finely chopped, scraping down the sides of the processor bowl with a rubber spatula. Store the excess garlic in a tightly sealed jar in the refrigerator.

PARSLEY: Parsley adds not only color but flavor to dishes. I prefer the flat-leaf (also called Italian) to curly leaf parsley: It has a richer, fuller taste.

OTHER FRESH HERBS: Fresh herbs are indispensable to my high-flavor, low-fat cooking. Imagine a tomato sauce without basil or a Thai noodle dish without cilantro. Most supermarkets carry a variety of fresh herbs in plastic pouches in the produce section. (And don't be afraid to substitute one kind of fresh herb for another.) Store fresh herbs loosely wrapped in a moist paper towel in an unsealed plastic bag in the refrigerator.

CHEESE: Cheese is quite high in saturated fat and cholesterol. For this reason (and unlike in most pasta books), you won't find much of it here. When I do use cheese, I choose a strong-flavored cheese such as feta or sharp cheddar, so that a little goes a long way. I'm not crazy about the no- and low-fat cheeses. I'd rather use a little real cheese occasionally than no-fat cheese every day.

GRATING CHEESE: The above notwithstanding, many pasta dishes would seem naked without a sprinkling of grated cheese. Two of the world's best grating cheeses are Parmigiano Reggiano and Pecorino Romano. The former is a part-skim cow's milk cheese from Emilia-

Romagna in northern Italy. The latter is a tangy sheep's-milk cheese made in Sardinia and around Rome. Both must be made in officially designated regions, according to strictly regulated procedures, to be allowed to bear their respective names. When one of the following recipes calls for "parmesan" or "romano cheese," take the trouble to buy real Parmigiano Reggiano and Pecorino Romano. (Look for the names stamped into the rind.) Grate the cheese fresh as you need it. The flavor is definitely worth the effort.

RICOTTA AND COTTAGE CHEESE: Here the cook has two types of reduced-fat cheeses to choose from: low fat and no fat. I much prefer the former to the latter in terms of texture and flavor. The following recipes will work with no-fat ricotta and cottage cheese, but if you can afford the fat grams, the low fat will give you better results.

SOUR CREAM: No-fat sour cream, on the other hand, is a good product with a pleasing flavor and texture. Unlike regular sour cream, it won't curdle when you boil it, so you can use it to make heart-healthy cream sauces. One good brand is Land O'Lakes.

STOCK: Another cornerstone of high-flavor, low-fat cooking, stock can be used in place of butter and cream in sauces and instead of or in addition to oil in salad dressings. Recipes for Chicken Stock and Vegetable Stock are found on pages 67 and 69. It's easy to make your own stock from scratch and also well worth the effort.

Finally, a word about some of the cooking techniques called for in this book.

To *shock-chill* means to immerse a cooked vegetable in a bowl of ice water. The sudden change of temperature intensifies and sets the vegetable's color and prevents overcooking.

When sautéing and stir-frying, use a nonstick utensil. You'll need less oil and foods will be less likely to stick.

*Stir-frying* is a high-heat Asian cooking method done in a wok. There are two keys to successful stir-frying: organization and high heat. Have all your ingredients measured out, cut, and lined up on a tray by the stove before you start. The actual cooking takes a matter of minutes, so you don't have time to run all over the kitchen looking for supplies.

Use a nonstick wok and heat to smoking before adding the oil. Keep the heat on high. Stir-frying is supposed to be fast. The high heat is needed to seal in the flavors properly.

I hope this book brings new excitement—and health—to your pasta repertory. I know that it did to mine!

# LOW-FAT PASTA SAUCES

## BASIC RED SAUCE
## WITH BASIL

*Here's a good, basic all-purpose red sauce—the sort consumed by the gallon by pasta lovers from Siena to Seattle.*
*Serve it over spaghetti, linguini, and other smooth noodles or with lasagna or baked stuffed shells.*
*For the best results, use canned plum tomatoes from Italy.*

2 tablespoons extra virgin olive oil
1 onion, minced (about 1 cup)
3 garlic cloves, minced
1 stalk celery, minced
¼ green bell pepper, minced
2 tablespoons tomato paste
1 28-ounce can imported peeled plum
   tomatoes

1½ teaspoons dried oregano
1 tablespoon balsamic vinegar
1 to 2 teaspoon sugar or honey (optional)
salt and freshly ground black pepper
12 to 16 fresh basil leaves, thinly slivered
   (optional)

1. Heat the olive oil in a large heavy sauce-pan. Add the onion, garlic, celery, and bell pepper and cook over medium heat until lightly browned, 6 to 8 minutes. Add the tomato paste after 4 minutes and cook it with the vegetables. Meanwhile, puree the tomatoes with their juices in a food processor or put them through a vegetable mill.

2. Stir the tomatoes with their juices, oregano, balsamic vinegar, sugar, if using, and salt and pepper into the vegetable mixture. Simmer the sauce, uncovered, over medium heat until thick and flavorful, about 10 to 15 minutes, stirring often. Stir in the basil, if using, and cook for 1 minute. Correct the seasoning, adding salt or sugar to taste.

**Note:** Refrigerated, the sauce will keep for 4 or 5 days. To put it up for future use, spoon the boiling sauce into canning jars that have been sterilized in boiling water for 10 minutes. Place sterile lids on top and screw on the caps. Invert the jars for 10 minutes (this sterilizes the lids), then reinvert.

*Makes about 4 cups. Serving is ½ to 1 cup*

74 CALORIES PER SERVING; 1 G PROTEIN; 5 G FAT; 1 G SATURATED FAT; 6 G CARBOHYDRATE; 153 MG SODIUM; 0 MG CHOLESTEROL

Analysis based on ½ cup serving

# BIG FLAVOR TOMATO SAUCE

*Here's a robust, rib-sticking tomato sauce for pasta that demands more substance. I prefer to use fresh tomatoes, but only when they're squishily ripe and in season. Otherwise, use good imported canned tomatoes. A recipe for homemade dried tomatoes can be found in my book* High-Flavor, Low-Fat Vegetarian Cookimg.

4 dried tomatoes
1 cup warm Vegetable Stock or Chicken
   Stock (see pages 67–69) or tomato juice
1½ tablespoons extra-virgin olive oil
1 medium onion, finely chopped (about 1 cup)
1 carrot, finely chopped
2 stalks celery, finely chopped
5 garlic cloves, minced
2 tablespoons tomato paste
4 large ripe tomatoes (about 2½ pounds), peeled,
   seeded, and finely chopped, with juices

1 tablespoon balsamic vinegar
2 teaspoons sugar or honey, or to taste
salt, freshly ground black pepper, and a pinch
   of cayenne pepper
1 tablespoon capers, drained
2 tablespoons chopped pitted black olives
2 anchovy fillets, finely chopped (optional)
¼ cup flat-leaf parsley, washed, stemmed, and
   finely chopped

1. Soak the dried tomatoes in the stock for 20 minutes, or until soft. Finely chop or sliver the dried tomatoes and return them to the stock. Set aside.

2. Heat the oil in a large saucepan. Cook the onion, carrot, celery, and garlic over medium heat until just beginning to brown, about 8 minutes. Add the tomato paste after 5 minutes and cook it with the vegetables.

3. Stir in the chopped tomatoes, stock with dried tomatoes, vinegar, sugar or honey, salt, pepper, and cayenne. Gently simmer the sauce until thick and very flavorful, 5 to 10 minutes, stirring as needed. Stir in the capers, olives, anchovies, and parsley and simmer for 2 minutes. Correct the seasoning, adding salt, vinegar, or sugar to taste. Refrigerated, the sauce will keep for 4 or 5 days.

*Makes about 5 cups. Serving is ½ to 1 cup*

85 CALORIES PER SERVING; 2 G PROTEIN; 4 G FAT; 0.5 G SATURATED FAT; 12 G CARBOHYDRATE; 179 MG SODIUM; 0 MG CHOLESTEROL

Analysis based on ½ cup serving

# TURKEY BOLOGNESE SAUCE

*Here's a rich, meaty red sauce that contains only a fraction of the fat found in a traditional bolognese. The secret is to use ground turkey and prosciutto instead of sausage and pork. If you buy the turkey preground, make sure it's freshly ground lean turkey breast. I've seen packaged ground turkey that contains as much fat as pork sausage! If you're in doubt, buy turkey breast and grind it yourself. For best results, use imported plum tomatoes.* **Note:** *A food processor works well for mincing the prosciutto and chopping the canned tomatoes.*

1 tablespoon olive oil
1 medium onion, finely chopped
3 garlic cloves, finely chopped
2 stalks celery, finely chopped
1 carrot, finely chopped
½ pound lean ground turkey breast
1 ounce prosciutto, minced
3 tablespoons tomato paste

¼ cup madeira
1 28-ounce can peeled tomatoes, finely chopped, with juices
1 tablespoon balsamic vinegar
1 teaspoon dried oregano
salt and freshly ground black pepper
3 tablespoons chopped fresh basil or flat-leaf parsley

1. Heat the olive oil in a large heavy saucepan (preferably nonstick). Add the onion, garlic, celery, and carrot and cook over medium heat until lightly browned, about 5 minutes.

2. Stir in the turkey and prosciutto and cook until the turkey is crumbly and nicely browned, 5 to 10 minutes, stirring and breaking up the meat with the edge of a wooden spoon. Add the tomato paste after 4 minutes. Add the madeira when the turkey is browned and bring to a boil.

3. Stir in the chopped tomatoes with juices, vinegar, oregano, and salt and pepper and simmer the sauce until richly flavored, about 10 minutes. Stir in the basil or parsley and cook for 1 minute. Correct the seasoning, adding salt, pepper, or vinegar as needed. Refrigerated, this sauce will keep for 3 to 4 days.

*Makes 4 cups. Serving is ½ to 1 cup*

119 CALORIES PER SERVING; 8 G PROTEIN; 6 G FAT; 1 G SATURATED FAT; 8 G CARBOHYDRATE; 246 MG SODIUM; 23 MG CHOLESTEROL

Analysis based on ½ cup serving

# LOW-FAT PESTO

*Pesto may seem like an unlikely candidate for a low-fat make-over. After all, three of its defining ingredients are olive oil, romano cheese, and pine nuts. To make a low-fat version, I substitute vegetable stock and no-fat sour cream for most of the oil. Most of the nuts have been replaced with chickpeas, while most of the cheese has been replaced with no-fat ricotta. I garnish the pasta with a few freshly toasted pine nuts (toasting enhances the flavor) and a little freshly grated romano cheese, so that these are the first flavors to hit the taste buds.*

4 cups fresh basil leaves, plus a few sprigs for garnish
½ cup flat-leaf parsley leaves
6 to 8 garlic cloves
½ cup cooked chickpeas
¼ cup no-fat ricotta cheese
¼ cup no-fat sour cream
about ¼ cup Vegetable Stock or Chicken Stock (see pages 67–69)

1 tablespoon extra virgin olive oil
1½ teaspoons fresh lemon juice
¼ teaspoon freshly grated lemon zest
salt and freshly ground black pepper to taste

FOR SERVING THE PESTO:
2 tablespoons lightly toasted pine nuts
2 to 4 tablespoons freshly grated romano cheese

Wash and stem the basil leaves and spin dry in a salad spinner. Place the basil, parsley, garlic, and chickpeas in a food processor and puree to a smooth paste. Work in the remaining ingredients, adding enough stock to obtain a thick but pourable sauce. Correct the seasoning, adding salt, pepper, or lemon juice to taste.

To serve, heat the pesto in a saucepan, but do not boil. Pour it over the cooked pasta. Sprinkle the pine nuts and grated romano on top and garnish with sprigs of basil. Refrigerated, the sauce will keep for 4 to 5 days, but it tastes best served the same day.

*Makes 2 cups. Serving is ⅓ to ½ cup*

93 CALORIES PER SERVING; 5 G PROTEIN; 5 G FAT; 1 G SATURATED FAT; 8 G CARBOHYDRATE; 112 MG SODIUM; 2 MG CHOLESTEROL
Analysis based on ½ cup serving

# ASIAN PEANUT SAUCE

*Many countries in Asia have a version of peanut sauce. Indonesians, for example, consume oceans of creamy coconut peanut sauce with their beloved satays (tiny kebabs). The Chinese crown noodle and chicken dishes, such as* dan dan *noodles and* peng peng *chicken, with a spicy sesame peanut sauce. The problem with these delectable sauces is the high-fat content of the peanuts. My low-fat version uses chickpeas to provide a nutty texture, with just a little peanut butter for flavor. Vegetable stock replaces the traditional coconut milk. Spoon the result over soba noodles, rice sticks, or spaghetti, and you'll have a quick, memorable Asian feast.*

3 scallions, trimmed and coarsely chopped
2 garlic cloves, coarsely chopped
2 shallots or ¼ cup red onion, peeled and
  coarsely chopped
1 tablespoon minced fresh ginger
1 to 2 jalapeño chilies, seeded and minced
  (for a hotter sauce, leave the seeds in)
2 cups cooked chickpeas, drained and rinsed
1 cup chopped tomatoes with juices (1 ripe
  tomato)
1 cup Chicken Stock or Vegetable Stock
  (see pages 67–69)

¼ cup chunky-style peanut butter
¼ cup tamari (see Note)
3 tablespoons fresh lime juice
2 tablespoons molasses
1 tablespoon honey
1 tablespoon tomato paste
1 teaspoon Asian hot sauce (see Note)
3 tablespoons finely chopped fresh cilantro
2 tablespoons black sesame seeds

1. Finely chop the scallions, garlic, shallots, ginger, and chilies in a food processor. Add the chickpeas and tomatoes and puree until smooth.

2. Place this mixture in a saucepan and stir in the stock, peanut butter, tamari, lime juice, molasses, honey, and tomato paste. Simmer the sauce until richly flavored and slightly thickened, about 5 minutes, whisking steadily.

Stir in the hot sauce, cilantro, and sesame seeds and simmer for 1 minute. Correct the seasoning, adding tamari, lime juice, or honey to taste. Refrigerated, the sauce will keep for up to a week.

**Note:** Tamari is a naturally fermented Japanese-style soy sauce. Look for it in natural foods stores, or use a good regular soy sauce, like Kikkoman. For a Thai-style peanut sauce, you can use fish sauce (which is made with pickled anchovies) instead of soy sauce. There are many Asian hot sauces. One good brand that's widely available is Sriracha from Thailand.

*Makes about 2 cups. Serving is ⅓ to ½ cup*

203 CALORIES PER SERVING; 9 G PROTEIN; 8 G FAT; 1 G SATURATED FAT; 27 G CARBOHYDRATE; 888 MG SODIUM; 0 MG CHOLESTEROL

Analysis based on ½ cup serving

# NOODLE SOUPS AND STEWS

## TIBETAN NOODLE STEW

*I first tasted this dish at the Tibetan Kitchen, a charming, tiny Manhattan restaurant. The noodle favored there is a short, open-sided tube called* gutse-ritu, *which closely resembles* cavatelli, *an Italian pasta widely available at gourmet shops.*

2 cups cavatelli or other thin tube-shaped pasta
1 tablespoon canola oil
2 onions, thinly sliced (about 1½ cups)
8 garlic cloves, thinly sliced
1 tablespoon minced fresh ginger
4 ounces lean lamb, thinly sliced (optional)
2 tomatoes, cut into ¼-inch dice

4 cups Chicken Stock or Vegetable Stock
  (see pages 67–69)
3 to 4 tablespoons tamari or soy sauce
  (see Note on page 6)
2 teaspoons hot paprika, or to taste
4 cups stemmed, washed spinach leaves

1. Cook the cavatelli in 4 quarts of boiling water until al dente, about 8 minutes. Drain in a colander, rinse with cold water until cool, and drain again.

2. Heat the oil in a wok or large saucepan, preferably nonstick. Add the onions, garlic, and ginger and cook over medium heat until nicely browned, about 5 minutes. Stir in the lamb, if using, and tomatoes and cook until the lamb loses its rawness, about 2 minutes.

3. Stir in the stock, tamari or soy sauce, and paprika and bring to a boil. Reduce the heat and simmer the stew until richly flavored and the lamb is tender, 5 to 10 minutes. Stir in the cavatelli and simmer for 2 minutes. Stir in the spinach leaves and cook until wilted, about 1 minute. Correct the seasoning, adding tamari or paprika to taste.
*Serves 4*

294 CALORIES PER SERVING; 12 G PROTEIN; 5 G FAT; 1 G SATURATED FAT; 53 G CARBOHYDRATE; 818 MG SODIUM; 0 MG CHOLESTEROL

# RICE NOODLE SOUP
# WITH ASIAN SEASONINGS

*Rice noodle soup is a mainstay of the Southeast Asian diet. Variations of this soulful bowlful are consumed at all hours of the day and night from Phnom Penh to Penang. This recipe doesn't come from a particular country, but features flavors from all over the region.* **Note:** *Don't be alarmed by what might seem an unsalubrious amount of oil; most of it is discarded.*

8 ounces rice sticks (see Note)
¼ cup canola oil
6 garlic cloves, peeled and thinly sliced
8 cups Chicken Stock or Vegetable Stock
   (see pages 67–69)
4 thin slices fresh ginger
1 bunch scallions, white part minced, green
   part finely chopped
2 star anise (optional)
2 cups cooked chicken, beef, or seafood,
   thinly sliced, or 6 ounces tofu, thinly sliced

freshly ground black pepper
4 to 5 tablespoons fish sauce (see Note), or to
   taste
3 cups mung bean sprouts
⅓ cup Thai or regular basil leaves
1 to 2 Thai or jalapeño chilies, sliced paper-
   thin (optional)
⅓ cup washed, stemmed cilantro
lime wedges for serving

1. Soak the rice sticks in cold water to cover until pliable, about 20 minutes.

2. Meanwhile, heat the oil in a wok to 350°F. Fry the sliced garlic until a light golden brown, about 30 seconds. Do not let the garlic brown too much or it will become bitter. Transfer the garlic with a slotted spoon to paper towels to drain. Let the oil cool and transfer it to a jar for use in other recipes. (A few drops of garlic oil add great flavor to salads and stews.) Wipe out the wok with a paper towel. Bring 4 quarts of

water to a boil in a large saucepan for cooking the noodles.

3. Place the stock, ginger, scallion whites, and star anise, if using, in the wok and bring to a boil. Reduce the heat and simmer for 5 minutes. Stir in the chicken, pepper, and fish sauce and simmer for 1 minute. Keep the broth hot, but do not boil.

4. Just before serving, drain the rice noodles. Cook them in the boiling water until tender, about 1 minute for thin rice sticks and 2 to 3

minutes for thick noodles. Drain the noodles in a colander and stir them into the broth. Correct the seasoning, adding pepper or fish sauce to taste. Stir in the bean sprouts, basil, and chilies and remove the pan from the heat. Ladle the soup into large bowls and sprinkle with the cilantro, scallion greens, and fried garlic. Garnish with lime wedges and serve at once.

**Note:** Rice sticks (also called rice noodles) are translucent noodles made from rice flour. Rice sticks come as thin as angel-hair pasta and as wide as fettuccine. Look for rice sticks at Asian markets, natural foods stores, and in the ethnic foods section of well-stocked supermarkets.

Fish sauce is a Southeast Asian condiment made from pickled anchovies. The best fish sauce comes from Thailand and Vietnam and is sold in glass bottles. Two good brands are Squid and Two Crabs. Fish sauce is available at Asian markets, gourmet shops, and in the ethnic foods section of most supermarkets.

*Serves 6 to 8 as a soup course,*
*4 as a main course*

202 CALORIES PER SERVING; 18 G PROTEIN; 7 G FAT; 2 G SATURATED FAT; 17 G CARBOHYDRATE; 150 MG SODIUM; 41 MG CHOLESTEROL

Analysis based on 4 servings

# COCONUT NOODLE STEW

*This colorful dish was inspired by Marnie's Noodle Shop, a postage stamp–size eatery in Greenwich Village that specializes in brimming bowls of Asian-style noodles. This recipe calls for chicken, but you can substitute seafood or make a vegetarian version by using shiitake mushrooms or other vegetables. Marnie's uses a thick, chewy, fresh udon-style noodle (see Pasta Primer, page 73), but any wheat noodle will do. (I've had great success with* perciatelli, bucatini, *and even* linguini.*)*

8 ounces boneless, skinless chicken breast
  (optional)
1 tablespoon canola oil
3 garlic cloves, minced
3 shallots, thinly sliced
1½ tablespoons minced fresh ginger
2 cups lite coconut milk (see Note)
4 cups Chicken Stock (see page 67)
1 tablespoon cornstarch

4 to 5 tablespoons Asian fish sauce (see Note
  on page 11) or soy sauce, or to taste
1 pound fresh udon noodles or 8 ounces dried
  udon (or other thick Asian wheat noodles)
  or perciatelli or bucatini
6 cups stemmed, washed fresh spinach
freshly ground black pepper
4 scallions, finely chopped

1. Wash the chicken breast, if using, and blot dry. Trim off any fat or sinew and cut the chicken breast widthwise into the thinnest possible slices.

2. Heat the oil in a nonstick wok or large saucepan. Add the garlic, shallots, and ginger and cook over medium heat until fragrant and just beginning to brown, about 2 minutes. Add the coconut milk and stock and bring to a rolling boil. Reduce the heat, add the chicken, and gently simmer until the chicken is cooked and the mixture is richly flavored, about 5 minutes.

3. Dissolve the cornstarch in the fish sauce in a small bowl. Stir this mixture into the broth and simmer for 1 to 2 minutes. The broth should thicken slightly.

4. Cook the noodles in 4 quarts of rapidly boiling water until tender, about 3 minutes for fresh noodles and 8 minutes for dried. Drain the noodles in a colander and add them to the coconut mixture. Simmer the noodles in the broth for 1 minute. Stir in the spinach and simmer until cooked, about 30 seconds. Add pepper to taste and, if needed, a little more fish sauce: The broth should be highly seasoned. Ladle the stew into bowls, sprinkle with scallions, and serve at once.

**Note:** Coconut milk, with its high saturated fat content, may seem like an unlikely ingredient for a low-fat cookbook, but the new "lite" coconut milk by A Taste of Thai contains only a third the fat found in regular coconut milk. A Taste of Thai Lite Coconut Milk is available in most gourmet shops. *Serves 4*

370 CALORIES PER SERVING; 13 G PROTEIN; 10 G FAT; 5 G SATURATED FAT; 58 G CARBOHYDRATE; 2,166 MG SODIUM; 0 MG CHOLESTEROL

# JAPANESE LUNCH NOODLES

*Noodles are one of Japan's national dishes—enjoyed day and night the way hamburgers and sandwiches are in the United States. Come lunchtime in Tokyo, office workers pour into noodle restaurants for their daily dose of soba (buckwheat noodles), udon (thick chewy wheat noodles), and ramen (thin wheat noodles). The broth and garnishes vary from dish to dish and restaurant to restaurant, but the joyful slurping remains the same. (You're supposed to make noise when you eat noodles in Japan.)*

**Note:** *Before you panic about finding Japanese noodles, the following recipe is delicious prepared with Italian-style pasta such as bucatini, linguini, or spaghetti. Other special ingredients are explained below. Meat eaters can substitute 6 to 8 ounces thinly sliced beef or chicken breast for the tofu.*

8 dried black mushrooms (see Note)
6 cups hot water or stock (see pages 67–69)
1 sweet potato (12 ounces), peeled and cut into ½-inch dice
1 leek, trimmed, washed, and thinly sliced
1 zucchini, cut widthwise into ¼-inch slices
4 cups stemmed kale leaves, cut crosswise into ½-inch strips
6 tablespoons miso (preferably hatcho-miso, see Note), or to taste

6 tablespoons mirin (see Note)
2 to 3 tablespoons honey or sugar, or to taste
1 pound fresh udon (or other wheat noodle) or 8 ounces dried (see Note)
10 ounces tofu (preferably extrafirm or firm silken), cut widthwise into ¼-inch slices
1 bunch scallions, trimmed and thinly sliced

1. Soak the mushrooms in 1 cup hot water or stock in a bowl until soft, about 20 minutes. Stem the mushrooms and cut each cap in quarters, reserving the soaking liquid. Bring 4 quarts of water to a boil in a large saucepan.

2. Place the mushroom soaking liquid and remaining stock in another large saucepan and bring to a boil. Add the sweet potato and leek

and simmer for 3 minutes. Add the zucchini, black mushrooms, and kale and cook until all the vegetables are tender, about 2 minutes more.

3. Remove the pan from the heat and stir in the miso, mirin, and honey or sugar. Stir until all the miso is dissolved. Correct the seasoning, adding miso or honey or sugar to taste: The broth should be highly seasoned. The recipe can

be prepared ahead to this stage. (If preparing ahead, don't boil the water for the noodles.)

4. Just before serving, cook the noodles in the boiling water until tender but not soft, about 3 minutes for fresh noodles, 8 minutes for dried. Drain the noodles in a colander. Stir them into the broth with the tofu and sliced scallions. Cook the noodles until thoroughly heated, but do not let the broth boil. (If it boils, you'll destroy some of the nutrients in the miso.) Serve the noodles at once, with a soup spoon and chopsticks.

To eat, raise the bowl to your mouth and slurp up the noodles and vegetables, using your chopsticks. Use the spoon for the broth. And make plenty of noise!

**Note:** Black mushrooms are dried shiitakes. Look for them at Asian markets, natural foods stores, and in the ethnic food section of most supermarkets.

Miso is a richly flavored and highly nutritious paste made from cultured soy beans and sometimes grains. My favorite type of miso for this recipe is hatcho-miso, a thick, dark, exceptionally flavorful miso that looks a little like fudge. (Hatcho takes its name from a famous miso shop located near my birthplace, Nagoya, Japan!) Hatcho-miso can be found at Japanese markets and most natural foods stores, but this dish is also delicious made with the more common red and white miso.

Mirin is a Japanese sweet rice wine. It's available at natural foods stores and many supermarkets. Cream sherry makes an acceptable substitute, but use a little less.

Udon are chewy, white, Japanese wheat noodles. If you live in a community with a large Japanese community, you can buy them fresh (or fresh frozen) at an Asian market. Dried udon are pearl white and are thicker than most noodles: They can be found at natural foods stores and at many supermarkets. But any type of cooked noodle will do. *Serves 4*

486 CALORIES PER SERVING; 19 G PROTEIN; 4 G FAT; 0 G SATURATED FAT; 91 G CARBOHYDRATE; 2,062 MG SODIUM; 0 MG CHOLESTEROL

# SPAETZLE SOUP

*Here's a twist on classic chicken noodle soup, made with tiny homemade egg noodles called spaetzle. (The word is a German diminutive for "sparrow," a reference to the noodle's birdlike shape.) Spaetzle are the only egg noodles I know of that can be made from start to finish from scratch in ten minutes, which makes them very popular around our house. (You'll need one special piece of equipment that is described in the Note to this recipe.) Spaetzle is traditionally served as a side dish; however, I like them in chicken soup. Think of the following as the ultimate comfort food.*

FOR THE SPAETZLE:
1 egg white
1 whole egg (or 2 more whites)
⅔ cup skim milk
¼ teaspoon freshly grated nutmeg, or to taste
¼ teaspoon freshly ground black pepper, or to taste
¾ teaspoon salt (optional)
1½ cups (approximately) unbleached all-purpose white flour
½ teaspoon canola oil

TO FINISH THE SOUP:
6 cups Chicken Stock (see page 67)
1 large or 2 medium carrots, cut into the finest possible dice
2 stalks celery, cut into the finest possible dice
1½ cups shredded cooked chicken (optional—see step 3 on page 68)
salt and freshly ground black pepper to taste
¼ cup coarsely chopped flat-leaf parsley

1. Combine the egg white and egg in a mixing bowl and whisk until smooth but not frothy. Whisk in the milk, seasonings, and enough flour to obtain a thick, sticky dough. (It should have the consistency of soft ice cream.)

2. Bring 4 quarts of water and the oil to a boil in a large, deep saucepan. Place the spaetzle machine over the pan, add the dough to the holder, and push back and forth to cut tiny droplets of dough into the water. Cook the spaetzle until the water returns to a boil and the noodles rise to the surface, about 1 minute. Remove the spaetzle with a skimmer or slotted spoon and transfer to a colander to drain. Rinse with cold water until cool. (This keeps the spaetzle from overcooking and removes the excess starch.) Continue cooking the spaetzle in this fashion until all the batter is used up. Drain well. The spaetzle can be prepared up to 48 hours ahead to this stage and refrigerated.

3. Just before serving, bring the chicken stock to a boil in a large saucepan. Add the car-

rot and celery and cook until soft, about 3 minutes. Stir in the chicken (if using) and spaetzle and cook until heated. Season the soup with salt and pepper to taste (it should be highly seasoned) and sprinkle with the parsley before serving.

**Note:** A spaetzle machine is a hand-held device consisting of a thin metal rectangle lined with rows of small holes, surmounted by a movable, open-topped box. The batter is placed in the box, which is slid back and forth over the metal plate. As it moves, tiny droplets of dough fall through the holes, forming tiny dumplings called spaetzle. Spaetzle machines can be purchased at most cookware shops.

*Serves 4 to 6*

234 CALORIES PER SERVING; 9 G PROTEIN; 3 G FAT; 1 G SATURATED FAT; 43 G CARBOHYDRATE; 93 MG SODIUM; 54 MG CHOLESTEROL

Analysis based on 4 servings

# PASTA SALADS

## PASTA PRIMAVERA SALAD

*This salad features a painter's palate of spring colors: the oranges of baby carrots, the greens of asparagus and fresh peas, the rose of new red potatoes. The choice is limited only to your imagination. Haricots verts are skinny French green beans. Look for them at gourmet shops and many supermarkets, or use the skinniest green beans you can find.*

2 cups short fusilli (or other curly pasta)
1½ tablespoons extra-virgin olive oil
4 ounces haricots verts, stem ends snapped off
6 ounces slender asparagus stalks
10 ounces fresh peas
6 ounces baby carrots
6 ounces baby red potatoes
12 basil leaves, plus a small sprig of basil for garnish

¼ cup finely chopped flat-leaf parsley
1 tablespoon tarragon vinegar or rice vinegar
1 tablespoon fresh lemon juice
½ teaspoon freshly grated lemon zest
1 garlic clove, minced
salt and freshly ground black pepper

1. Bring 4 quarts of salted water to a boil for cooking the pasta and vegetables. Cook the fusilli until al dente, about 8 minutes. Using a wire skimmer or slotted spoon, transfer the pasta to a colander, rinse under cold water until cool, and drain well. Transfer the fusilli to a mixing bowl and toss with olive oil. Return the water to a boil.

2. Cut the haricots verts into 2-inch pieces. Snap the fibrous ends off the asparagus and cut the stalks into 2-inch pieces. Shell the peas. Cut the carrots and new potatoes in half lengthwise. Cook the haricots verts, asparagus, and peas in the boiling water until crispy-tender, about 2 minutes. Drain the vegetables and transfer to a bowl of ice water. (The sudden cold helps

*Pasta Primavera Salad*

intensify the colors.) Cook the carrots and potatoes in the boiling water until tender, 4 to 6 minutes. Drain the vegetables and transfer to the bowl of ice water. Drain all the vegetables in a colander, blot dry on paper towels, and add them to the salad.

3. Just before serving, cut the basil leaves crosswise into ¼-inch strips. Add the basil, parsley, vinegar, lemon juice, lemon zest, garlic, and salt and pepper to the salad and toss to mix. Correct the seasoning, adding lemon juice, salt, or pepper to taste. The salad should be highly seasoned. Garnish with the basil sprig and serve at once.                                    *Serves 4*

373 CALORIES PER SERVING; 13 G PROTEIN; 7 G FAT; 1 G SATURATED FAT; 66 G CARBOHYDRATE; 35 G SODIUM; 0 G CHOLESTEROL

# RIGATI, TOMATO, AND ARUGULA SALAD

*Here's a pasta salad perfect for summer entertaining: It's pretty to look at and quick and easy to prepare.*
*The arugula makes it both refreshing and a little spicy. Rigati are ridged pasta tubes. If unavailable,*
*you can use another tube-shaped pasta such as penne or ditali.*

2 cups rigati
3 tablespoons balsamic vinegar
2 tablespoons Chicken Stock or Vegetable
   Stock (see pages 67–69)
1½ tablespoons extra-virgin olive oil
1 garlic clove, minced
salt and freshly ground black pepper

2 cups ripe cherry tomatoes, stemmed and cut
   in half
2 bunches arugula, cut crosswise into 1-inch
   ribbons
¼ cup pitted black olives
1 tablespoon capers, drained
½ teaspoon hot pepper flakes (optional)

1. Cook the rigati in 4 quarts of rapidly boiling water until al dente, about 8 minutes. Drain the pasta in a colander, refresh under cold water, and drain well again.

2. Combine the vinegar, stock, oil, garlic, and salt and pepper to taste in an attractive salad bowl. Whisk until the salt crystals are dissolved. Stir in the pasta, tomatoes, arugula, olives, ca-pers, and pepper flakes, if using. Toss to mix. Correct the seasoning, adding vinegar or salt to taste: The pasta should be highly seasoned.

**Note:** This salad tastes best served within 10 minutes of tossing. You can have all the ingredients ready, but try to toss it at the last minute.

*Serves 4*

283 CALORIES PER SERVING; 8 G PROTEIN; 8 G FAT; 1 G SATURATED FAT; 46 G CARBOHYDRATE; 106 MG SODIUM; 0 MG CHOLESTEROL

# SANTA FE SALAD (WAGON WHEELS WITH ROASTED CHILIES AND CORN)

*One of the most distinctive of Italy's pastas is* ruote di carro, *"cartwheels." This set me thinking about the covered wagons of America's Wild West and before long I imagined a wagon-wheel pasta salad garnished with such Southwestern flavorings as chili peppers, roasted corn, and cilantro. You can certainly add 1 to 2 cups diced cooked chicken to this salad and serve it as a light main course.* **Note:** *For a quicker salad, you can skip roasting the peppers and simply dice them.*

**FOR THE DRESSING:**
4 tablespoons no-fat sour cream
2 to 3 tablespoons fresh lime juice
2 tablespoons Chicken Stock or Vegetable
   Stock (see pages 67–69)
2 tablespoons ketchup
1 tablespoon extra-virgin olive oil (optional),
   plus 1 teaspoon for grilling the corn
1 tablespoon chili powder
1 garlic clove, minced
salt and freshly ground black pepper

**TO FINISH THE SALAD:**
2 cups wagon-wheel pasta (ruote di carro)
4 poblano chilies or 2 green bell peppers
   (see Note)
3 ears corn, shucked
½ red bell pepper, cut into ¼-inch dice
   (about ½ cup)
½ red onion, cut into ¼-inch dice (about
   ½ cup)
½ cup finely chopped fresh cilantro, plus a
   few sprigs for garnish
1 to 2 jalapeño chilies, seeded and finely
   chopped (for a hotter salad, leave the
   seeds in)

1. Combine the ingredients for the dressing in a large attractive serving bowl and whisk until smooth.

2. Cook the wagon wheels in 4 quarts of boiling water until al dente, 8 to 10 minutes.

Drain the wagon wheels in a colander, refresh under cold water, and drain well. Stir the pasta into the dressing. Preheat a barbecue grill or broiler to high.

3. Roast the chilies over a high flame until

charred on all sides, about 8 minutes. Wrap the chilies in wet paper towels and let cool. Brush the corn with the reserved 1 teaspoon oil and season with salt and pepper. Grill the corn until nicely browned on all sides, turning often, about 8 minutes. Transfer the corn to a cutting board and cut the kernels off the cobs. (The easiest way to do this is to lay the ears flat on the cutting board and make lengthwise cuts with a chopping knife.)

4. Scrape the burnt skin off the chilies, cut the chilies in half, and remove the seeds and stems. Cut the chilies into ¼-inch strips and add them to the pasta with the corn. Stir in the red bell pepper, onion, cilantro, and jalapeños. Correct the seasoning, adding salt, chili powder, and/or lime juice to taste: The salad should be highly seasoned. Garnish the salad with cilantro sprigs before serving.

**Note:** The poblano is a dark green, mildly hot, elongated triangle-shaped chili traditionally used by Mexicans to make *chiles rellenos*. Look for them at Hispanic grocery stores, gourmet greengrocers, and many supermarkets. *Serves 4*

314 CALORIES PER SERVING; 10 G PROTEIN; 3 G FAT; 0 G SATURATED FAT; 64 G CARBOHYDRATE; 139 MG SODIUM; 0 MG CHOLESTEROL

# CURRIED ORZO SALAD

*Orzo is the noodle that thinks it's rice. Tiny and elongated, with tapered ends, it certainly looks like rice. But there's no mistaking its delicate texture and wheaty flavor: It's really a type of pasta.*

**FOR THE DRESSING:**
½ cup non-fat yogurt
1 tablespoon fresh lemon juice
1 tablespoon soy sauce
1 tablespoon curry powder
1 tablespoon mustard oil or sesame oil
    (optional; see Note)
2 teaspoons brown sugar
1 to 2 slices candied ginger, finely chopped
salt and freshly ground black pepper
3 scallions, white part minced, green part
    finely chopped

**TO FINISH THE SALAD:**
2 cups orzo
½ pound haricots verts or green beans, ends
    snapped off and cut into 1-inch pieces
salt
½ pound cooked shrimp (or chicken)
1 red bell pepper, cored, seeded, and finely
    diced
8 pitted dates, thinly sliced
1 large ripe tomato

1. In a large mixing bowl combine the ingredients for the dressing, minus the scallion greens, and whisk until mixed. Correct the seasoning, adding salt and pepper to taste: The dressing should be highly seasoned.

2. Cook the orzo in 4 quarts of boiling water until al dente, about 6 minutes. Drain in a colander, rinse with cold water until cool, and drain well. Stir the orzo into the dressing.

3. Cook the haricots verts in at least 1 quart boiling salted water until crispy-tender, about 2 minutes. Drain the beans in a colander, shock-chill with ice water, and drain well. Cut the shrimp into ½-inch dice, leaving 4 whole shrimp for garnish. Stir the haricots verts, shrimp, pepper, and dates into the salad.

4. Make a tomato rose: Cut the peel off the tomato in a continuous strip about 1 inch wide, using a sharp paring knife. Roll this strip into a tight roll and stand it on end: You should wind up with what looks like a rose. Set the rose aside for garnish. Cut the tomato in half widthwise and wring out the seeds. Cut the tomato into ¼-inch dice and stir it into the salad.

5. Just before serving, taste the salad for seasoning, adding salt, lemon juice, or curry powder

to taste: The salad should be highly seasoned. Transfer the salad to a platter or serving bowl and garnish with the tomato rose, whole shrimp, and chopped scallion greens.

**Note:** To shock-chill means to immerse a boiled vegetable in a bowl of ice water. The sudden change of temperature intensifies the vegetable's color.

Mustard oil is a peppery oil pressed from mustard seeds and available in Indian markets. Sesame oil is made from roasted sesame seeds. When buying sesame oil, be sure you choose a dark (roasted) oil; a good brand is Kadoya from Japan. *Serves 4*

361 CALORIES PER SERVING; 65 G PROTEIN; 2 G FAT; 0 G SATURATED FAT; 65 G CARBOHYDRATE; 424 MG SODIUM; 111 MG CHOLESTEROL

# ASIAN NOODLE SALAD

*This colorful salad is great for a picnic or a summer buffet. There are several possibilities for noodles: you could use Chinese egg noodles, Japanese wheat noodles (such as ramen or udon), soba (Japanese buckwheat noodles), or even Western spaghetti.*

8 ounces pre-steamed Chinese egg noodles, dried wheat noodles, spaghetti, or bucatini
1 teaspoon sesame oil
8 ounces asparagus
salt
8 ounces snow peas, ends snapped off and strings removed
1 red bell pepper, cored, seeded, and cut into matchstick slivers
1 yellow bell pepper, cored, seeded, and cut into matchstick slivers

1 15-ounce can baby corn, drained
6 scallions, white part minced, green part thinly sliced on the diagonal

FOR THE DRESSING:
1 clove garlic, minced
3 tablespoons toasted sesame seeds
¼ cup rice vinegar
¼ cup honey
1 tablespoon sesame oil
freshly ground black pepper

1. Cook the noodles in 4 quarts boiling water until al dente, 6 to 8 minutes. Drain the noodles in a colander, rinse with cold water until cool, and drain well. Transfer the noodles to a large mixing bowl and toss with 1 teaspoon sesame oil.

2. Snap the fibrous ends off the asparagus and cut the stalks sharply on the diagonal into 2-inch pieces. Cook the asparagus in 2 quarts boiling salted water until crispy-tender, about 3 minutes. With a slotted spoon, transfer the asparagus to a colander and shock-chill with ice water (see Note). Drain well. Cook, drain, and chill the snow peas the same way. (They'll need about 1 minute of cooking.)

3. Prepare the dressing. Mash the garlic and half the sesame seeds in an attractive serving bowl. Add the vinegar, honey, remaining 1 tablespoon sesame oil, salt, and pepper, and whisk until the salt crystals are dissolved. Correct the seasoning, adding salt or vinegar to taste: the dressing should be highly seasoned.

4. Add the noodles, asparagus, snow peas, peppers, baby corn, scallion whites, and half the scallion greens to the dressing and toss to mix. Sprinkle the remaining sesame seeds and scallion greens on top and serve at once.

**Note:** Shock-chilling means immersing or rinsing a vegetable in ice water. The sudden cold interrupts the cooking process and intensifies the vegetable color.

*Serves 4 to 6*

414 CALORIES PER SERVING; 13 G PROTEIN; 10 G FAT; 1 G SATURATED FAT; 72 G CARBOHYDRATE; 231 MG SODIUM; 41 MG CHOLESTEROL

Analysis based on 4 servings

# SAUTÉED, STUFFED, AND BAKED PASTAS

## PEPPER CONFETTI MACARONI AND CHEESE

*Diced red, green, and yellow bell peppers give this macaroni the festive look of confetti.*
*The flavor of the vegetables enables you to reduce the amount of cheese.*

8 ounces macaroni or rigatoni

FOR THE SAUCE:
1 tablespoon olive oil
1 large onion, finely chopped
3 garlic cloves, minced
2 red bell peppers
2 yellow bell peppers
1 green bell pepper (or 2 ancho chilies for a
   little more spice) (see Note on page 23)
¼ cup flour
3 cups skim milk

1 to 1½ cups crumbled feta cheese (or other
   strong-flavored cheese)
2 tablespoons chopped fresh dill (or 1
   tablespoon dried)
1 tablespoon Dijon-style mustard
salt and freshly ground black pepper
dash cayenne pepper and freshly grated
   nutmeg

vegetable spray oil
½ cup toasted bread crumbs

1. Bring 4 quarts of lightly salted water to a rolling boil in a large pot. Cook the macaroni until al dente, about 8 minutes. Drain the macaroni in a colander, rinse with cold water to cool, and drain well. Preheat the oven to 400°F.

2. Meanwhile, prepare the sauce. Heat the olive oil in a large sauté pan, preferably nonstick. Add the onion, garlic, and peppers and cook over medium heat until the vegetables are soft and aromatic, but not brown, about 4 minutes. Stir in

*Pepper Confetti Macaroni and Cheese*

the flour and cook for 1 minute more. Stir in the skim milk and bring to a boil, stirring steadily. Simmer the sauce until thickened, about 1 minute. Stir in the cheese, dill, mustard, salt and pepper, and cayenne and nutmeg to taste. The sauce should be highly seasoned.

3. Stir the macaroni into the sauce. Spoon the mixture into an attractive 8- by 12-inch baking dish you've lightly sprayed with oil. Sprinkle the top with bread crumbs. Bake the macaroni and cheese until bubbling, crusty, and golden brown, 30 to 40 minutes.   *Serves 6*

408 CALORIES PER SERVING; 18 G PROTEIN; 13 G FAT; 7 G SATURATED FAT; 55 G CARBOHYDRATE; 665 MG SODIUM; 40 MG CHOLESTEROL

# BOW TIES WITH SALMON, SPINACH, AND BLACK MUSHROOMS

*Here's a colorful dish loaded with protein, vitamins, and healthful fish oils. I like the smoky flavor you get from Chinese dried black mushrooms, which are available at most supermarkets. But you can also use fresh shiitakes or even button mushrooms if you omit the soaking in step 1.*

8 Chinese black mushrooms (see Note), fresh shiitakes, or large button mushrooms
8 ounces pasta bow ties (farfalle)

FOR THE SAUCE:
¼ cup Chicken Stock or Vegetable Stock (see pages 67–69)
3 tablespoons oyster sauce (see Note)
3 tablespoons rice wine or sake
1 tablespoon soy sauce
½ teaspoon chili oil or hot sauce (optional)

2 teaspoons sugar
2 teaspoons cornstarch

1 tablespoon canola oil
3 garlic cloves, minced
3 scallions, white part minced, green part finely chopped
2 teaspoons minced fresh ginger
12 ounces boneless, skinless salmon fillets, cut into ¼- by 1-inch slivers
5 cups fresh spinach leaves (about 4 ounces), stemmed and washed

1. Soak the black mushrooms in 1 cup warm water until soft, about 20 minutes. Drain the mushrooms, remove and discard the stems, and quarter the caps.

2. Meanwhile, bring 4 quarts of lightly salted water to a boil in a large pot for cooking the pasta. Cook the bow ties until al dente, about 8 minutes. Drain the bow ties in a colander, rinse with cold water to cool, and drain well. Combine the ingredients for the sauce in a small bowl and stir to mix.

3. Just before serving, heat a wok or large nonstick frying pan to smoking. Swirl in the oil. Add the garlic, scallion whites, and ginger. Stir-fry over high heat until fragrant but not brown, about 15 seconds. Add the salmon and mushrooms and stir-fry until the fish is almost cooked, 1 to 2 minutes.

4. Stir the ingredients of the sauce to redissolve the sugar and cornstarch. Add the sauce to the wok with the spinach and bring to a boil. Stir in the bow ties and cook until the spinach is

cooked and the noodles are thoroughly heated, about 1 minute. Sprinkle the dish with the scallion greens and serve at once.

**Note:** Black mushrooms are dried shiitake mushrooms. Oyster sauce is a tangy brown sauce flavored with oysters and used often in Cantonese cooking. (If unavailable, use soy sauce.) Both are available at Asian markets, natural foods stores, and in the ethnic foods sections of most supermarkets.                    *Serves 4*

375 CALORIES PER SERVING; 22 G PROTEIN; 8 G FAT; 1 G SATURATED FAT; 52 G CARBOHYDRATE; 834 MG SODIUM; 16 MG CHOLESTEROL

# LASAGNA ROLL-UPS WITH SPINACH AND BASIL

*Here's a contemporary twist on an age-old favorite: lasagna in easy-to-serve individual rolls rather than in messy layers. This dish tastes best when made with fresh spinach. To wash spinach, immerse it in a large bowl of cold water, agitate it with your fingers, and transfer it with your fingers to a colander. Pour off the dirty water (not over the spinach!) and repeat until the spinach is clean.*

12 lasagna noodles (with ruffled edges)
4 cups Big Flavor Tomato Sauce (see page 3)
   or Basic Red Sauce with Basil (see page 1),
   or your favorite low-fat spaghetti sauce

FOR THE FILLING:
1 pound fresh spinach, stemmed and washed
3 garlic cloves, coarsely chopped
4 scallions, trimmed and coarsely chopped
1 bunch basil, stemmed

2 cups (15-ounce container) of low-fat ricotta
   cheese
¼ cup dry bread crumbs
2 egg whites
salt and freshly ground black pepper to taste
freshly grated nutmeg and cayenne pepper to
   taste

vegetable spray oil

1. Cook the lasagna noodles in 4 quarts of boiling salted water until al dente, about 8 minutes. Drain the noodles in a colander, rinse with cold water, and drain well. Spread the noodles on sheets of plastic wrap and cover with more plastic wrap. Prepare the Big Flavor Tomato Sauce or other sauce of your choice.

2. Prepare the filling. Cook the spinach in a large pot in ½ inch of boiling salted water until wilted and tender, about 2 minutes. Transfer the spinach to a colander and rinse with cold water to cool. Wring all the liquid out of the spinach by tightly squeezing it between your hands. Preheat the oven to 400°F.

3. Transfer the spinach to a food processor with the garlic, scallions, and basil. Grind the mixture to a fine paste. Add the ricotta cheese and puree. Add the bread crumbs, egg whites, salt and pepper, and nutmeg and cayenne. The filling should be highly seasoned.

4. Spread a lasagna noodle on the work surface, narrow end toward you. Using a rubber spatula, spread 2 to 3 tablespoons filling on top of the noodle. Roll up the noodle and place it,

seam side down, in an 8- by 12-inch baking dish lightly coated with spray oil. Continue filling and rolling the noodles in this fashion until all are used up. Spoon the tomato sauce on top. The recipe can be prepared ahead to this stage and refrigerated. (Be sure to let the lasagna come to room temperature before baking.)

5. Bake the lasagna until the sauce is bubbling and the rolls are thoroughly heated, about 30 minutes. (To test the internal temperature of the rolls, insert a slender skewer. It should come out hot to the touch.) Serve at once.

*Makes 12 rolls, enough to serve 12
as an appetizer or 6 as a main course*

400 CALORIES PER SERVING; 17 G PROTEIN; 10 G FAT; 1 G SATURATED FAT; 62 G CARBOHYDRATE; 134 MG SODIUM; 10 MG CHOLESTEROL

Analysis based on 6 servings

# SHRIMP RAVIOLI
# WITH ROASTED RED PEPPER SAUCE

*East meets West in this recipe—ravioli filled with gingery shrimp mousse and served on a colorful pepper sauce. For speed and convenience, I make the ravioli with wonton wrappers, which are widely available in the produce section of most supermarkets. (Good brands include Leasa and Frieda's.) The purist can certainly use homemade pasta. If you're in a hurry, you can omit the pepper sauce and serve the ravioli in scallion broth (see step 1 on page 60).*

FOR THE SHRIMP MOUSSE:
1 8-ounce can water chestnuts, drained
8 ounces peeled, deveined shrimp
1 garlic clove, minced
1 scallion, minced
2 teaspoons minced fresh ginger
1 teaspoon soy sauce
½ teaspoon sugar

salt and freshly ground black pepper to taste

Roasted Red Pepper Sauce (see page 36)
1 package wonton wrappers (36 three-inch squares)
¼ cup coarsely chopped fresh cilantro or scallion greens

1. Finely chop the water chestnuts in a food processor and transfer to a mixing bowl. Puree the shrimp in the food processor. Add the garlic, scallion, ginger, soy sauce, sugar, and salt and pepper and puree again. Stir the shrimp mousse into the water chestnuts. Correct the seasoning, adding salt to taste: The mixture should be highly seasoned. (*Note:* To taste the mixture for seasoning without eating raw shrimp, cook a tiny bit of mousse on the end of a spoon in boiling water.) Prepare the Roasted Red Pepper Sauce. Bring 4 quarts of water to a boil in a large pot for cooking the ravioli.

2. Spread a few wonton wrappers on a work surface. Lightly brush the edges with water. Place a teaspoon of shrimp mousse in the center of each and fold it in half on the diagonal. Starting at one end and continuing to the other, seal the edges by gently patting with your fingers. It's important to make a hermetic seal. Assemble the remaining ravioli in this fashion. Transfer the finished ravioli to a cake rack.

3. Cook the ravioli in the boiling water until the pasta is translucent and the filling is firm and

white, about 2 to 3 minutes. Drain the ravioli in a colander. Spoon the pepper sauce on plates or a platter and arrange the ravioli on top. Sprinkle with cilantro or scallion greens and serve at once. *Makes about 36 ravioli, which will serve 9 as an appetizer or 4 to 6 as an entree*

234 CALORIES PER SERVING; 17 G PROTEIN; 5 G FAT; 1 G SATURATED FAT; 30 G CARBOHYDRATE; 157 MG SODIUM; 139 MG CHOLESTEROL

Analysis based on 4 servings

## ROASTED RED PEPPER SAUCE

*This is the one dish in this book you can burn. Indeed, charring the bell peppers gives them an inimitable sweet-smoky flavor that makes the sauce delicious enough to eat straight off a spoon. A yellow bell pepper sauce can be made the same way.*

2 large red bell peppers
1 garlic clove, chopped
1 cup Vegetable Stock or Chicken Stock (see pages 67–69), or as needed
1½ tablespoons balsamic or wine vinegar, or to taste

1 tablespoon extra-virgin olive oil
¼ teaspoon saffron threads soaked in 1 tablespoon warm water (optional)
salt and freshly ground black pepper
pinch of cayenne pepper

1. Roast the peppers over high heat on a barbecue grill, under a broiler, or directly over a gas or electric burner until charred and black on all sides. Turn as necessary with tongs: The whole process should take 8 to 10 minutes. Wrap the charred peppers in wet paper towels and let cool.

2. Scrape the charred skin off the peppers, using the tip of a paring knife. (Don't worry if you leave a few charred bits behind.) Core the peppers and scrape out the seeds, working over a strainer and bowl to catch the juices.

3. Place all the ingredients for the sauce (including the pepper juices) in a blender and puree until smooth. The sauce should be pourable: If too thick, add a little more stock. Correct the seasoning, adding salt, vinegar, or cayenne to taste: The sauce should be highly seasoned.

*Makes 1 ½ cups*

43 CALORIES PER SERVING; 1 G PROTEIN; 3 G FAT; 0 G SATURATED FAT; 3 G CARBOHYDRATE; 3 MG SODIUM; 0 MG CHOLESTEROL

# SWEET NOODLE PUDDING
# WITH APPLES

*Kugel is a Jewish noodle pudding. This one owes its fruity flavor to the addition of grated apples, almond extract, and cardamom. It's also the only recipe in this book that contains butter (just a little), which you can certainly omit if you wish. I dedicate this recipe to my friend, the late Bob Ginn, who loved kugel so much he once served seven different types at a Passover seder!*

1 cup golden or black raisins
1 cup apple cider or apple juice
8 ounces flat egg noodles
2 Granny Smith or other firm apples
2 cups no-fat sour cream
5 egg whites
1 egg (to further reduce the fat, you can
   replace the egg with 2 more egg whites)
1 tablespoon vanilla extract
1 teaspoon almond extract
1 teaspoon ground cardamom
1 teaspoon ground cinnamon
1 teaspoon grated lemon zest

2 cups low-fat large-curd cottage cheese
⅓ to ½ cup light brown sugar or Succanat
   (see Note)

vegetable spray oil

FOR THE TOPPING:
½ cup cinnamon graham cracker crumbs,
   regular graham cracker crumbs, or bread
   crumbs
2 tablespoons white sugar or Succanat
1 to 2 tablespoons butter (optional)

1. Preheat the oven to 350°F. Plump the raisins in the apple cider for 30 minutes. Drain well. Cook the noodles in 4 quarts rapidly boiling salted water until a little shy of al dente, about 6 minutes. Drain the noodles in a colander, rinse with cold water, and drain again. Wash, core, and coarsely grate the apples on the large-hole side of a grater. (I don't generally bother to peel the apples.) Squeeze the grated apples between your fingers to wring out the excess liquid.

2. In a mixing bowl, combine the sour cream, egg whites, egg, vanilla and almond extracts, cardamom, cinnamon, and lemon zest and whisk until smooth. Stir in the cottage cheese, sugar, noodles, raisins, and grated apples. Correct the seasoning, adding sugar or cinnamon to taste.

3. Spoon the noodle mixture into an 8- by

12-inch baking dish lightly sprayed with oil. Sprinkle the top with the graham cracker crumbs and sugar and dot with butter, if using.

4. Bake the kugel until set and golden brown, about 50 minutes. Let the kugel cool for 5 minutes, then cut into squares for serving.

**Note:** Succanat is freeze-dried sugarcane juice. It contains all the nutrients that are normally removed when sugar is refined. It also has an interesting malty flavor. Succanat can be found at natural foods stores.                    *Serves 8 to 10*

362 CALORIES PER SERVING; 17 G PROTEIN; 3 G FAT; 1 G SATURATED FAT; 65 G CARBOHYDRATE; 435 MG SODIUM; 54 MG CHOLESTEROL

Analysis based on 8 servings

# COUSCOUS "PILAF"

*Couscous is the noodle that thinks itself a grain. These tiny pellets of pasta are enjoyed throughout North Africa, where they're steamed and served as an accompaniment to stews. I like to think of the following recipe as a couscous pilaf—generously endowed with a colorful assortment of dried fruits and nuts. Serve it by itself as a light entree or as an accompaniment to roast chicken or grilled lamb or seafood.*

1 tablespoon extra-virgin olive oil
1 medium onion, finely chopped
2 stalks celery, finely chopped
2 garlic cloves, minced
¼ cup walnut pieces or pine nuts
2 cups couscous (10-ounce box)
2½ cups hot Vegetable Stock or Chicken
 Stock (see pages 67–69)

1½ cups mixed pitted dried fruits (including
 dates, raisins, prunes, cherries, and/or
 apricots), diced
1 cinnamon stick
salt and freshly ground black pepper
3 tablespoons finely chopped flat-leaf parsley
 or chives

1. Heat the oil in a large heavy saucepan. Add the onion, celery, garlic, and walnuts and cook over medium heat until lightly browned, about 4 minutes. Stir in the couscous and cook until lightly toasted, about 1 minute.

2. Stir in the stock, dried fruits, cinnamon stick, and salt and pepper. Cover the pan and let stand for 5 minutes. Fluff the couscous with a fork, discard the cinnamon stick, and correct the seasoning with salt and pepper. Sprinkle the pilaf with the parsley and serve at once.　　*Serves 4*

591 CALORIES PER SERVING; 16 G PROTEIN; 9 G FAT; 1 G SATURATED FAT; 115 G CARBOHYDRATE; 37 MG SODIUM; 0 MG CHOLESTEROL

# PASTA WITH SAUCE

## SPICY MUSSEL CAPELLINI

*This colorful dish, a study in red and black, recalls an Italo-American favorite: fra diavolo. You can also prepare it with shrimp or scallops, or any type of seafood: you'll need about 1 pound. Capellini (also known as capelli d'angelo, "angel hair") is a super-thin spaghetti. I've called for a range of pepper flakes: ¼ teaspoon will give you a mild heat; ½ teaspoon, a mild sweat. My favorite vermouth for this dish is Noilly Prat.*

2 pounds mussels
2 cups dry white vermouth or white wine
1 tablespoon extra-virgin olive oil
¼ to ½ teaspoon hot pepper flakes, or more
1 large onion, finely chopped (about 1½ cups)
4 garlic cloves, thinly sliced
1 green bell pepper, cored, seeded, and finely chopped
2 stalks celery, finely chopped

2 tablespoons tomato paste
4 ripe tomatoes, seeded and finely chopped
1 tablespoon wine or balsamic vinegar, or to taste
1 teaspoon fresh or dried thyme
½ cup finely chopped fresh parsley, preferably flat leaf
salt and freshly ground black pepper
8 ounces capellini or other long, thin dried pasta

1. Scrub the mussels, discarding any with cracked shells or shells that fail to close when tapped. Remove any threads found at the hinges of the mussel shells. (A needle-nose pliers works well for this task.) Bring the wine to a boil. Add the mussels, tightly cover the pan, and cook over high heat until the mussel shells open, 4 to 6 minutes, stirring once or twice. Transfer the mussels to a colander with a slotted spoon. Strain the cooking liquid into a measuring cup. You'll need 2 cups. (Extra broth can be frozen for future use in any recipe that calls for fish stock or

clam broth.) Bring 4 quarts of water to a boil for cooking the pasta.

2. Heat the olive oil with the hot pepper flakes in a large sauté pan. Add the onion, garlic, pepper, and celery. Cook the mixture, uncovered, over medium high heat, stirring often, until golden brown, about 6 minutes. Add the tomato paste after 3 minutes and cook with the vegetables.

3. Increase the heat to high and stir in the tomatoes. Cook until the tomato liquid begins to evaporate, about 1 minute. Stir in the 2 cups of mussel liquid, vinegar, thyme, half of the parsley, and salt and pepper. Briskly simmer the sauce until thick and flavorful, about 5 minutes. Stir in the mussels and correct the seasoning, adding salt, vinegar, or hot pepper flakes to taste. The mixture should be highly seasoned. The recipe can be prepared ahead to this stage.

4. Meanwhile, cook the capellini in the boiling water until al dente, 4 to 6 minutes. Drain in a colander and transfer to a platter. Spoon the mussels and sauce on top and sprinkle with the remaining parsley. Serve at once.

**Note:** For an even richer taste, you can simmer the cooked pasta in the sauce for a minute or two before serving. *Serves 4*

417 CALORIES PER SERVING; 18 G PROTEIN; 7 G FAT; 1 G SATURATED FAT; 65 G CARBOHYDRATE; 292 MG SODIUM; 18 MG CHOLESTEROL

# CUBAN SPAGHETTI

*No book of mine would be complete without at least one recipe from our friend and recipe tester extraordinaire, Elida Proenza. Here's how a fine Cuban cook makes spaghetti.*

1 tablespoon olive oil
1 small onion, finely chopped
2 garlic cloves, minced
½ red bell pepper, finely chopped
½ teaspoon cumin
½ teaspoon oregano
1 large ripe tomato, finely chopped

1 tablespoon capers, drained
10 pitted black olives, cut in half
¼ cup chopped cilantro or flat-leaf parsley
1 8-ounce can tomato sauce
salt and freshly ground black pepper
1 pound shrimp, peeled and deveined
8 ounces spaghetti or other long, thin pasta

1. Bring 4 quarts of water to a boil in a large pot for cooking the spaghetti. Heat the olive oil in a large sauté pan. Add the onion, garlic, pepper, cumin, and oregano and cook over medium heat until just beginning to brown, about 4 minutes, stirring often. Add the tomato, capers, olives, and half the cilantro and cook until the tomato liquid begins to evaporate, about 2 minutes.

2. Add the tomato sauce and salt and pepper and simmer the mixture until rich and flavorful, about 5 minutes. Stir in the shrimp and simmer until cooked, about 3 minutes. Correct the seasoning, adding salt, pepper, and a little more cumin if necessary. The sauce should be highly seasoned.

3. Meanwhile, cook the spaghetti in the boiling water until al dente, about 8 minutes. Drain in a colander. Stir the spaghetti into the sauce and simmer for 1 minute. Sprinkle with the remaining cilantro and serve at once.

*Serves 4*

509 CALORIES PER SERVING; 27 G PROTEIN; 8 G FAT; 1 G SATURATED FAT; 83 G CARBOHYDRATE; 610 MG SODIUM; 122 MG CHOLESTEROL

# PENNE PIPERADE

*Piperade is a Basque specialty, a stunning sauté of red, green, and yellow bell peppers scrambled with eggs and fortified with paprika. Why not replace the eggs with pasta, I reasoned, as I set out to create a low-fat version. You can certainly omit the ham if you're trying to reduce your meat intake.*

4 cups penne (see Pasta Primer, page 72)

FOR THE SAUCE:
1 tablespoon extra-virgin olive oil
1 green bell pepper, cored, seeded, and cut
   into penne-size pieces
1 red bell pepper, cored, seeded, and cut
   into penne-size pieces
1 yellow bell pepper, cored, seeded, and cut
   into penne-size pieces
1 medium onion, thinly sliced

3 garlic cloves, thinly sliced
2 to 3 thin slices prosciutto, Black Forest
   ham, or Canadian bacon, cut into thin
   slivers (1 to 2 ounces—optional)
2 large ripe tomatoes, finely chopped (with
   juices)
1 to 3 teaspoons hot paprika
salt and freshly ground black pepper
½ cup chopped flat-leaf parsley
1 ounce feta, Manchego, or other sheep's
   milk cheese (optional)

1. Cook the penne in at least 4 quarts of rapidly boiling water until al dente, about 8 minutes. Drain the pasta in a colander, refresh under cold water, and drain well again.

2. Heat the olive oil in a large sauté pan, preferably nonstick. Add the peppers, onion, garlic, and prosciutto and cook over medium heat until lightly browned, about 5 minutes. Stir in the tomatoes, paprika, salt and pepper, and half the parsley. Cook until the tomatoes yield their juices and the mixture is moist and saucy, about 5 minutes.

3. Stir in the penne and bring to a boil. Correct the seasoning, adding salt or paprika to taste. The mixture should be highly seasoned. Sprinkle the penne with the remaining parsley. Grate the cheese on top, if using, and serve at once.                                    *Serves 4*

277 CALORIES PER SERVING; 9 G PROTEIN; 5 G FAT; 1 G SATURATED FAT; 51 G CARBOHYDRATE; 16 MG SODIUM; 0 MG CHOLESTEROL

# GNOCCHI WITH TURKEY SAUSAGE AND MUSTARD GREENS

*This dish is fairly brimming with flavor. Turkey sausage can be found at gourmet shops and most supermarkets. (Choose the leanest you can find.) Grilling gives the sausage a smoky flavor and allows you to cook out the excess fat. The arugula adds color and heat. Gnocchi is a tiny Italian potato dumpling, of course, but there's also a gnocchi pasta that looks like an elongated ridged shell.*

12 ounces turkey sausage (2 links)
8 ounces gnocchi pasta (or small shells)
1 tablespoon extra-virgin olive oil
1 large onion, finely chopped
2 stalks celery, finely chopped
1 red bell pepper, cored, seeded, and diced
2 garlic cloves, minced
1 teaspoon ground coriander

½ teaspoon ground cumin
½ cup dry white vermouth or white wine
2 ripe tomatoes, cut into ½-inch dice
2 cups Chicken Stock (see page 67)
salt and freshly ground black pepper
1 large bunch arugula (3 to 4 cups), stemmed, washed, and cut crosswise into ½-inch strips
3 to 4 tablespoons grated romano cheese

1. Bring 4 quarts water to a boil in a large pot for cooking the pasta. Preheat the grill or broiler. Prick the sausage all over with a pin or toothpick. (This allows the steam to escape.) Grill or broil the sausage until cooked, about 4 minutes per side. Thinly slice the sausage on the diagonal. Transfer the slices to a plate lined with paper towels and blot dry.

2. Cook the gnocchi pasta in the rapidly boiling water until al dente, about 8 minutes. Drain the pasta in a colander.

3. Meanwhile, heat the olive oil in a large non-stick frying pan. Cook the onion, celery, pepper, garlic, coriander, and cumin over medium heat until lightly browned, about 4 minutes. Stir in the vermouth and bring to a boil. Stir in the tomatoes, sausage, stock, salt, and pepper and simmer the sauce until richly flavored and slightly reduced, about 4 minutes.

4. Stir in the pasta and cook until thoroughly heated and the stock is partially absorbed, about 2 minutes. Stir in the arugula and serve at once, with the cheese on the side for sprinkling. *Serves 4*

477 CALORIES PER SERVING; 27 G PROTEIN; 13 G FAT; 4 G SATURATED FAT; 57 G CARBOHYDRATE; 839 MG SODIUM; 61 MG CHOLESTEROL

# PASTA PIQUANTE

*This dish started as a low-fat version of Italy's classic* aglio e olio *(pasta with oil and garlic). Most of the oil was replaced with chicken stock. To make up for the lost richness, I started adding intense flavorings: anchovies, capers, olives, garlic, and hot peppers. The result is a far cry from the original, but it sings with flavor!*

FOR THE SAUCE:
1½ tablespoons extra-virgin olive oil
6 to 8 garlic cloves, cut widthwise into paper-
   thin slices
1 small can anchovy fillets, drained, blotted
   dry, and cut widthwise into ¼-inch pieces
½ teaspoon hot pepper flakes
2 tablespoons red wine vinegar, or to taste
3 tablespoons capers, drained
8 pitted oil-cured or Kalamata olives, thinly
   sliced

1 large or 2 small ripe tomatoes, peeled,
   seeded, and cut into ¼-inch dice
1 teaspoon grated lemon zest
1 cup chopped flat-leaf parsley
2 cups Chicken Stock (see page 67)
salt and freshly ground black pepper

10 ounces linguini
¼ to ½ cup freshly grated romano cheese for
   serving

1. Bring 4 quarts of water to a boil in a large pot for cooking the pasta.

2. Heat the olive oil in a large nonstick skillet. Add the garlic, anchovy pieces, and hot pepper flakes and cook over medium heat until the garlic is golden brown, about 2 minutes. Add the vinegar and bring to a boil. Stir in the capers, olives, tomato, lemon zest, half the parsley, and chicken stock and bring to a boil. Simmer the sauce until richly flavored, about 3 minutes. Correct the seasoning, adding salt or vinegar to taste.

3. Meanwhile, cook the linguini in the rapidly boiling, lightly salted water until just shy of al dente, about 7 minutes. Drain the pasta in a colander.

4. Stir the linguini into the sauce and cook it over high heat until thoroughly heated and some of the stock is absorbed, about 2 minutes. Serve it in bowls (the sauce is quite soupy), with the remaining parsley on top. Serve at once, with grated cheese on the side for sprinkling.

*Serves 4*

411 CALORIES PER SERVING; 17 G PROTEIN; 11 G FAT; 3 G SATURATED FAT; 62 G CARBOHYDRATE; 825 MG SODIUM; 19 MG CHOLESTEROL

# PAPPARDELLE WITH EXOTIC MUSHROOMS

*When I was growing up, mushrooms meant button mushrooms. My, how times have changed! Today's cook has access to a dazzling range of exotic mushrooms, many available at your local supermarket. For the following recipe you can use shiitakes, creminis, portabellos, oyster mushrooms, chanterelles, porcinis, and/or morels. Better still, use a combination. Pappardelle are wide ( ½ to 1 inch) egg noodles. The dish would also be good with fettuccine.*

1 pound fresh exotic mushrooms
1½ tablespoons extra-virgin olive oil
3 garlic cloves, minced
2 shallots, minced
¼ cup madeira or cognac
¾ cup Vegetable Stock or Chicken Stock
  (see pages 67–69)

¾ cup no-fat sour cream
½ cup finely chopped flat-leaf parsley
salt and freshly ground black pepper
1 pound fresh pappardelle or 8 ounces dried
¼ cup freshly grated Parmigiano Reggiano
  (parmesan) cheese for serving

1. Bring 4 quarts of water to a boil in a large pot for cooking the pasta. Trim off the ends of the mushroom stems and gently wipe any dirt off the caps with a damp cloth. Thinly slice the mushrooms.

2. Heat the olive oil in a large nonstick skillet over medium heat. Add the garlic and shallots and cook over medium heat until soft but not brown, about 2 minutes. Increase the heat to high, add the mushrooms, and cook until the mushrooms are soft, about 3 minutes. Stir in the madeira and boil until reduced by half, about 2 minutes.

3. Stir in the stock, sour cream, and half of the parsley and bring to a boil. Simmer the mixture until thick and well flavored, about 10 minutes. Correct the seasoning, adding salt and pepper to taste.

4. Meanwhile, cook the pappardelle until al dente. Fresh pasta will take 2 to 3 minutes to cook; dried pasta about 8 minutes. Drain the pasta well in a colander and stir it into the mushroom sauce. Cook for 1 to 2 minutes, stirring well, to heat the pasta and thoroughly coat it with sauce. Sprinkle the remaining parsley on top and serve at once, with the cheese on the side for sprinkling. *Serves 4*

349 CALORIES PER SERVING; 14 G PROTEIN; 10 G FAT; 2 G SATURATED FAT; 48 G CARBOHYDRATE; 210 MG SODIUM; 54 MG CHOLESTEROL

# A NEW SPAGHETTI
# WITH CLAMS

*Here's a New England twist on classic Italian spaghetti alle vongole (spaghetti with clams). The potatoes and Canadian bacon recall Yankee chowder, and they add substance to the dish, enabling you to reduce the oil and omit the traditional butter. For best results, use fresh littlenecks or other small clams.*
**Note:** *Canned clams will work in a pinch. (You'll need two 6.5-ounce cans.)*

36 littleneck clams (the smaller the better)
1 tablespoon extra-virgin olive oil
3 garlic cloves, minced
1 ounce thinly sliced Canadian bacon or
   smoked ham
¼ teaspoon hot pepper flakes

½ cup dry white vermouth or dry white wine
1 cup bottled clam broth or fish stock
1 baking potato (about ½ pound), peeled and
   cut into ¼-inch dice
8 ounces spaghetti, spaghettini, or linguini
½ cup chopped flat-leaf parsley

1. Bring 4 quarts of water to a boil in a large pot for cooking the pasta. Scrub the clam shells under cold water with a stiff bristle brush.

2. Heat the olive oil in a large nonstick skillet. Add the garlic and cook over medium heat until fragrant but not brown, about 1 minute. Stir in the bacon and pepper flakes and cook for 1 minute. Add the vermouth and bring to a boil. Add the clam broth and bring to a boil. Stir in the potatoes and clams, tightly cover the pan, and cook until the shells open and the potatoes are tender, about 8 minutes.

3. Cook the spaghetti in the boiling water until al dente, about 8 minutes. Drain the pasta in a colander. Stir it into the sauce and cook until thoroughly heated and coated with sauce, about 2 minutes. Stir in the parsley and serve at once.

**Note:** For a spicier dish, you can substitute 2 cups slivered arugula leaves for the parsley.

*Serves 4*

394 CALORIES PER SERVING; 18 G PROTEIN; 6 G FAT; 1 G SATURATED FAT; 61 G CARBOHYDRATE; 263 MG SODIUM; 60 MG CHOLESTEROL

# FETTUCCINE WITH CAVIAR
# AND SMOKED SALMON

*Here's an extravagant pasta dish that's perfect for New Year's Eve. (But don't wait for New Year's to try it!)*
*A hot smoked salmon (kippered or Pacific Northwest–style) is lower in fat than Scottish smoked*
*salmon or nova, but the latter may be used in moderation. Salmon caviar (sometimes called salmon roe)*
*is available at Japanese markets, gourmet shops, and most supermarkets.*

FOR THE SAUCE:
1 tablespoon extra-virgin olive oil
¼ cup minced shallots (3 or 4 whole shallots)
½ cup dry white vermouth
1 cup bottled clam broth or fish stock
1 cup no-fat sour cream
4 to 8 ounces smoked salmon, flaked or
    thinly slivered

1 teaspoon grated lemon zest
2 tablespoons chopped dill or flat-leaf parsley
salt and freshly ground black pepper

TO FINISH THE PASTA:
8 ounces dried fettuccine or 1 pound fresh
    fettuccine
2 ounces salmon caviar

1. Prepare the sauce: Heat the oil in a large nonstick skillet. Add the shallots and cook over medium heat until soft, but not brown, about 3 minutes. Add the vermouth and bring to a boil. Boil the vermouth until reduced by half. Whisk in the clam broth and sour cream and briskly simmer the sauce until thickened to the consistency of heavy cream. Stir in the smoked salmon, lemon zest, and parsley and simmer until the sauce has a rich smoky flavor, 1 to 2 minutes. Stir in salt and pepper to taste.

2. Cook the pasta in 4 quarts of rapidly boiling water until al dente. Dried pasta will take about 8 minutes to cook; fresh pasta, 2 to 3 minutes. Drain the pasta well in a colander and stir it into the smoked salmon sauce. Cook until thoroughly heated, 1 to 2 minutes. Dot the fettuccine with the caviar and serve at once.

*Serves 6 as an appetizer, 4 as an entree*

368 CALORIES PER SERVING; 18 G PROTEIN; 9 G FAT; 2 G SATURATED FAT; 44 G CARBOHYDRATE; 677 MG SODIUM; 139 MG CHOLESTEROL

Analysis based on 4 servings

# TEX-MEX
# ARRABBIATA

*The name of this Italian dish literally means "angry." The more hot pepper flakes you add,
the "angrier" the sauce will be. That set me thinking about another part of the world
where emotions are expressed with chili peppers. The result is Tex-Mex Arrabbiata.
There are several possibilities for pasta here, including fusilli, penne rigate
(ridged penne), spaghetti, or eliche (helixes).*

FOR THE SAUCE:
1 28-ounce can imported peeled tomatoes
1 tablespoon extra-virgin olive oil
3 garlic cloves, finely chopped
2 ounces thinly sliced Canadian bacon, cut
    into ¼-inch slivers
1 to 4 jalapeño or serrano chilies, thinly
    sliced (for a milder arrabbiata, seed the
    chilies and finely chop)
2 tablespoons fresh lime juice

1 teaspoon chili powder, preferably chipotle
    (see Note)
½ cup washed cilantro leaves, plus 4 sprigs
    for garnish
salt and freshly ground black pepper

8 ounces long fusilli or other dried
    pasta
3 to 4 tablespoons freshly grated romano
    cheese

1. Prepare the sauce: Drain the tomatoes in a colander, reserving the juice. Coarsely chop the tomatoes: You should have about 2 cups. Bring 4 quarts of water to a boil in a large pot for cooking the pasta.

2. Heat the olive oil in a large nonstick skillet. Add the garlic and cook over medium heat until fragrant but not brown, about 1 minute. Stir in the bacon and chilies and cook until lightly browned, about 3 minutes. Stir in the chopped tomatoes with 1 cup juice and bring to a boil. Reduce the heat and simmer the sauce until richly flavored, about 3 minutes. Stir in the lime juice, chili powder, half the cilantro, and salt and pepper and cook for 30 seconds. Correct the seasoning, adding salt or lime juice to taste.

3. Cook the fusilli in the boiling water until al dente, about 8 minutes. Drain in a colander. Stir the fusilli into the sauce and cook until

thoroughly heated and coated with sauce, about 2 minutes. Stir in the remaining cilantro and sprinkle the grated cheese on top.

**Note:** My favorite chili powder for this recipe is chipotle, made with dried smoked jalapeño chilies. Chipotle chili powder can be found at Mexican markets and gourmet shops.          *Serves 4*

431 CALORIES PER SERVING; 17 G PROTEIN; 9 G FAT; 2 G SATURATED FAT; 71 G CARBOHYDRATE; 567 MG SODIUM; 12 MG CHOLESTEROL

# ASIAN NOODLE DISHES

## NONYA NOODLES

*Nonya is the Malay word for "grandmother." The term refers to a unique Singaporean style of cooking that combines Chinese cooking techniques, such as stir-frying, with the Malay love of spices and coconut milk. To reduce the fat, I use a "lite" coconut milk; one good brand is made by A Taste of Thai.*

salt
4 ounces long beans (see Note), green beans, or haricots verts
2 large carrots, peeled and thinly sliced on the diagonal
8 ounces pre-steamed Chinese egg noodles (see Note) or dried wheat noodles
4 garlic cloves, finely chopped
3 shallots, finely chopped
4 teaspoons finely chopped fresh ginger

1 to 3 hot chilies, finely chopped (for milder noodles, seed the chilies)
1 tablespoon canola oil
¾ cup "lite" coconut milk
¾ cup Chicken Stock or Vegetable Stock (see pages 67–69)
3 tablespoons Asian fish sauce or soy sauce (see Notes on pages 7 and 11)
freshly ground black pepper
3 tablespoons finely chopped scallion greens

1. Bring 4 quarts of salted water to a boil in a large pot for cooking the vegetables and noodles.

2. Snap the ends off the beans. If using long beans, cut them into 3-inch pieces. Cook the beans in the boiling water until crispy-tender,

about 2 minutes. Transfer the beans to a colander with a slotted spoon, rinse with ice water, and drain again. Cook, drain, and chill the carrots the same way.

3. Add the noodles to the boiling water and cook until tender, 6 to 8 minutes. Drain the noo-

dles in a colander, rinse with cold water, and drain again.

4. Puree the garlic, shallots, ginger, and chilies in a mortar and pestle or food processor. Heat the oil in a nonstick wok or frying pan. Add the garlic paste and stir-fry until fragrant, about 2 minutes. Stir in the coconut milk, stock, fish sauce, and pepper. Boil the mixture until slightly thickened and very flavorful, about 2 minutes.

5. Stir in the noodles and simmer until most of the sauce is absorbed, 2 to 3 minutes. Stir in the long beans and carrots and cook until heated. Correct the seasoning, adding fish sauce or pepper to taste. Sprinkle the noodles with the scallion greens and serve at once.

**Note:** Long beans are Asian green beans that grow up to two feet in length. Look for them in Asian and West Indian markets or use regular green beans.

Chinese egg noodles are a thin yellow pasta made from flour, eggs, and a little oil. Most supermarkets carry pre-steamed egg noodles, which are partially cooked and conveniently packaged in sealed plastic bags. One widely available brand is Leasa. Other possibilities for noodles include udon, ramen, or even fettuccine.   *Serves 4*

305 CALORIES PER SERVING; 10 G PROTEIN; 8 G FAT; 2 G SATURATED FAT; 49 G CARBOHYDRATE; 808 MG SODIUM; 49 MG CHOLESTEROL

# VIETNAMESE NOODLE STIR-FRY

*Here's a quick, home-style dish from central Vietnam. I learned how to make it at a cozy restaurant called*
*Vietfood, run by a soft-spoken couple named Tan and Gam Thi Doan in the Boston suburb of Watertown.*
*Vegetarians can omit the pork and shrimp, substituting 4 ounces thinly sliced tofu.*

8 ounces pre-steamed Chinese egg noodles
(see Note on page 54) or dried wheat
noodles
1 tablespoon canola oil
2 garlic cloves, minced
3 scallions, white part minced, green part
thinly sliced
1 tablespoon minced fresh lemongrass or 1
teaspoon grated lemon zest (optional)
1 onion, thinly sliced
2 carrots, cut into matchstick slivers
(julienned)

4 ounces lean pork or chicken breast, thinly
sliced
12 small or 8 medium shrimp, peeled and
deveined
3 tablespoons fish sauce or soy sauce
(see Notes on pages 7 and 11), or to taste
2 cups mung bean sprouts
12 fresh basil leaves or mint leaves, thinly
sliced
2 to 3 tablespoons coarsely chopped dry
roasted peanuts

1. Cook the noodles in 4 quarts of rapidly boiling water until al dente, 6 to 8 minutes for pre-steamed noodles, 8 minutes for dried noodles. Drain in a colander, rinse with cold water, and drain again.

2. Just before serving, heat a wok (preferably nonstick) over a medium-high flame. Swirl in the oil. Add the garlic, scallion whites, lemongrass, if using, and onion and stir-fry until fragrant but not brown, about 30 seconds. Add the carrots, pork, and shrimp and stir-fry until cooked, 1 to 2 minutes.

3. Stir in the noodles and fish sauce and stir-fry until the noodles are heated, about 2 minutes. If using grated lemon zest, add it now. Stir in the bean sprouts and basil and cook until the sprouts are just tender, about 30 seconds. Correct the seasoning, adding fish sauce to taste. Sprinkle with the scallion greens and peanuts and serve. *Serves 4*

367 CALORIES PER SERVING; 22 G PROTEIN; 9 G FAT; 1 G SATURATED FAT; 50 G CARBOHYDRATE; 895 MG SODIUM; 107 MG CHOLESTEROL

# THAI NOODLE "BOUILLABAISSE"

*The Thai love of explosive flavors is apparent in this dish—a cross between stir-fried noodles and bouillabaisse. The delicate interplay of sweet (honey and peanuts), sour (lime juice), salty (fish sauce or soy sauce), and aromatic (chilies and basil) will send you rushing back for seconds. The noodle of choice is a rice stick (see Note), but you can also use cooked linguini or fettuccine. This recipe can be prepared with any type of seafood, from shrimp or fish (you'll need about 1 pound) to the selection listed below. Vegetarians can replace the seafood with tofu and cooked vegetables.*

8 ounces rice sticks
2 pounds mussels or clams in the shell
1 cup rice wine or white wine
½ pound shrimp
½ pound squid or scallops

FOR THE SAUCE:
1 cup mussel juice (or chicken or vegetable stock)
5 tablespoons Asian fish sauce or soy sauce (see Notes on pages 7 and 11)
5 tablespoons lime juice
3 tablespoons honey or sugar

TO FINISH THE NOODLES:
1 tablespoon canola oil
1 to 3 Thai or jalapeño chilies, minced (for a milder dish, seed the chilies before mincing)
3 garlic cloves, minced
1 tablespoon minced fresh ginger
3 scallions, white part minced, green part finely chopped
1 carrot, thinly sliced on the diagonal
4 ounces snow peas, strings and stems removed
2 cups fresh mung bean sprouts
1 bunch basil, stemmed
2 to 3 tablespoons coarsely chopped dry roasted peanuts

1. Soak the rice sticks in cool water to cover, for 20 minutes.

2. Scrub the mussels, discarding any with cracked shells or shells that fail to close when tapped. Remove any tufts of threads found at the hinges of the mussel shells. (A needle-nose pliers works well for this task.) Bring the wine to a boil. Add the mussels, tightly cover the pan, and cook over high heat until the mussel shells open, 4 to 6 minutes, stirring once or twice. Transfer

the mussels to a colander with a slotted spoon. Shell most of them, reserving 12 in the shell for garnish. Strain the cooking liquid into a measuring cup. You'll need 1 cup. (Extra broth can be frozen for future use in any recipe that calls for fish stock or clam broth.) Peel and devein the shrimp. Thinly slice the squid or scallops.

3. Combine the ingredients for the sauce and stir until mixed.

4. Just before serving, heat a large wok (preferably nonstick) or skillet over high heat and swirl in the oil. Add the chilies, garlic, ginger, and scallion whites and stir-fry until fragrant, about 15 seconds. Add the carrot, snow peas, and shrimp and stir-fry for 2 minutes, or until the shrimp starts to turn pink.

5. Stir in the sauce and bring to a boil. Add the rice sticks and squid and cook until the noodles are almost soft, 2 to 3 minutes. Stir in the bean sprouts and basil leaves and stir-fry until the sprouts lose their rawness and all the seafood is cooked, about 1 minute more. Stir in the mussels. Transfer the Thai noodle "bouillabaisse" to a platter and sprinkle with the chopped peanuts and scallion greens. Serve at once.

**Note:** Rice sticks are noodles made from rice flour and water. They come in a broad range of widths: from capellini-thin strands to fettuccine-thick ribbons. I like a rice stick that's 1/8 to 1/4 inch wide for this recipe. Thin rice sticks will need only a minute of cooking, thick rice sticks, 2 to 4 minutes. If rice noodles are unavailable, you can use spaghetti or linguini. (You'll need about 8 ounces of dried.)          *Serves 4*

514 CALORIES PER SERVING; 35 G PROTEIN; 9 G FAT; 2 G SATURATED FAT; 74 G CARBOHYDRATE; 1,624 MG SODIUM; 211 MG CHOLESTEROL

# MR. KEE'S
# LAMB CHOW MEIN

*One of my favorite restaurants in Boston's Chinatown is barely a restaurant at all. King Fung Garden consists of a single dining room with five tables in a building so rickety, it looks as though it might blow down in the next snowstorm. The kitchen is even smaller and more rickety, but from its narrow confines emerge some of the most wondrous noodle dishes I've eaten on three continents. The man behind this culinary pleasure is Mr. Fung Kee, a quiet septuagenarian who was born in northern China, trained in Hong Kong, and has spent the last two decades in Boston. Mr. Kee uses a variety of fresh wheat noodles—some as thick as green beans. If you live in an area with a large Chinese population, you may be able to find them. This recipe has been designed for the steamed egg noodles sold in plastic bags in supermarket produce sections.* **Note:** *Partially freezing the lamb helps facilitate slicing.*

8 ounces pre-steamed Chinese egg noodles
   (see Note on page 54)
½ pound lean leg of lamb

FOR THE SAUCE:
½ cup Chicken Stock or Vegetable Stock (see
   pages 67–69)
3 tablespoons soy sauce
3 tablespoons Chinese rice wine or dry sherry
1 tablespoon honey or sugar
1 to 3 tablespoons chili paste or hot bean
   paste (optional; see Note)

1 tablespoon cornstarch
salt and freshly ground black pepper

1 tablespoon canola oil
3 garlic cloves, minced
1 tablespoon minced fresh ginger
3 scallions, white part minced, green part cut
   on the diagonal into ½-inch slivers
1 cup thinly sliced green cabbage or nappa
   (Chinese cabbage)
1 carrot, cut into matchstick slivers
1 cup snow peas, stems and strings removed

1. Cook the noodles in 4 quarts of boiling water in a large pot until tender, 6 to 8 minutes. Drain the noodles in a colander and rinse with cold water.

2. Cut the lamb across the grain into paper-thin slices. Combine the ingredients for the sauce in a small bowl and stir until the honey and cornstarch are dissolved.

3. Heat a large wok (preferably nonstick) over a high flame and swirl in the oil. Add the garlic, ginger, and scallion whites and stir-fry until fragrant but not brown, about 15 seconds.

Add the lamb and stir-fry until pink, 1 to 2 minutes. Add the cabbage, carrot, and snow peas and continue cooking until the vegetables are tender, about 1 minute. Stir in the noodles. Stir the sauce to redissolve the cornstarch and add it to the noodles. Stir-fry the mixture until thoroughly heated, about 2 minutes. The sauce should boil. Sprinkle the noodles with the scallion greens and serve at once.

**Note:** Chili paste and hot bean paste are fiery Chinese condiments. Both contain chilies, salt, and garlic; the latter contains soy beans as well. I've made them optional; by now you've probably gathered I love fiery food. Both are available at Asian markets and in the ethic foods sections of most supermarkets.    *Serves 4*

393 CALORIES PER SERVING; 21 G PROTEIN; 8 G FAT; 1 G SATURATED FAT; 59 G CARBOHYDRATE; 370 MG SODIUM; 91 MG CHOLESTEROL

# CHILLED BUCKWHEAT NOODLES WITH SPICY SCALLION BROTH

*I first tasted this dish thirty-five thousand feet above sea level aboard a Singapore Airlines plane bound for Tokyo. It came in a high-tech plastic tray with a large compartment for the coils of noodles, two small ones for the chopped scallions and wasabi, plus a small bowl of cold broth and a tiny bag of slivered seaweed. I can't think of a more refreshing treat on a warm summer day—or a better restorative after fifteen hours of flying!*

**FOR THE BROTH:**
2 cups cold Chicken Stock or Vegetable Stock (see pages 67–69), or beef stock
½ cup mirin (Japanese sweet rice wine—see Note)
5 tablespoons rice vinegar
5 tablespoons soy sauce or fish sauce (see Notes on pages 7 and 11)

8 ounces dry soba noodles (preferably green soba) (see Note)
2 sheets nori seaweed (see Note)
1 tablespoon wasabi (see Note)
4 scallions, finely chopped

1. In a mixing bowl combine the stock, mirin, vinegar, and soy or fish sauce and stir to mix. Correct the seasoning, adding more of these ingredients if your taste requires. The broth should be highly seasoned. Transfer the broth to four small bowls or Asian teacups.

2. Cook the soba in 4 quarts of rapidly boiling water until just tender, about 8 minutes. Drain the noodles in a colander, chill in a bowl of ice water, and drain again. Roll the noodles into coil-shaped bundles and transfer to plates or a platter.

3. Cut the nori seaweed into matchstick slivers and place in a small bowl. In another small bowl, mix the wasabi with 1 tablespoon hot water to form a thick paste and let stand for 5 minutes. Place the scallions in a third small bowl.

4. To serve, sprinkle the noodles with the slivered seaweed. Have each person stir scallions and wasabi to taste into his/her broth. Dip a small coil of noodles in the broth with chopsticks, then eat.

**Note:** This recipe is simplicity itself to make, but you'll need a few special ingredients, all of which can be found at a natural foods store or Japanese market. Soba are Japanese buckwheat noodles:

Green soba are colored with green tea. (You don't really taste the tea, but the noodles are really pretty.)

Mirin is a sweet Japanese rice wine. If unavailable, you can substitute sake and a little sugar or cream sherry.

Nori is pressed dried laver seaweed. You've undoubtedly seen it at Japanese restaurants, where it's used as a wrapping for sushi. Wasabi, another sushi ingredient, is Japanese horseradish.

The traditional broth for this dish is dashi, which is made with dried bonita flakes. To simplify the recipe, I've called for chicken (or vegetable or beef) stock, but dashi is easy to make. (Follow the recipe on the back of the package.)

*Serves 4*

237 CALORIES PER SERVING; 11 G PROTEIN; 1 G FAT; 0.1 G SATURATED FAT; 48 G CARBOHYDRATE; 1,795 MG SODIUM; 0 MG CHOLESTEROL

# MEE GORING—MUSLIM-STYLE NOODLES WITH LAMB

*Singapore may well be the world's noodle capital. The residents of this tiny nation eat noodles for breakfast, lunch, dinner, midnight snack, and at just about any time in between. Mee goring is a Muslim specialty of Indonesian origin, a popular dish at Newton Circus and Singapore's other hawker centers. Chicken or tofu can be substituted for the lamb.*

8 ounces pre-steamed Chinese egg noodles (see Note on page 54) or dried wheat noodles

FOR THE SAUCE:
¼ cup ketchup
¼ cup Singaporean or Thai chili sauce (see Note)
2 tablespoons soy sauce
1 tablespoon chili paste (optional—see Note)
2 teaspoons sugar
salt and freshly ground black pepper to taste

1 tablespoon canola oil
3 garlic cloves, minced
1 onion, thinly sliced
8 ounces lean lamb, very finely chopped or minced
2 cups thinly sliced nappa (Chinese cabbage) or Savoy or green cabbage
2 cups snow peas, strings and stems removed
2 cups mung bean sprouts
1 cucumber, peeled, seeded, and cut into fine dice
¼ cup cilantro leaves or chopped scallion greens

1. Cook the noodles in 4 quarts of boiling water until tender, 6 to 8 minutes for fresh or pre-steamed noodles, 8 minutes for dried noodles. Drain the noodles in a colander, rinse with cold water until cool, and drain again.

2. Combine the ingredients for the sauce in a small bowl and whisk until smooth.

3. Heat a large wok (preferably nonstick) over a high flame and swirl in the oil. Add the garlic and onion and stir-fry until just beginning to brown, about 1 minute. Add the lamb, cabbage, and snow peas and stir-fry until the lamb is cooked, about 2 minutes. Add the noodles, bean sprouts, and sauce and stir-fry until the noodles are thoroughly heated, 2 to 3 minutes. Correct the seasoning, adding chili sauce or soy sauce. The mixture should be highly seasoned. Sprinkle the noodles with the diced cucumber and cilantro and serve at once.

**Note:** Chili sauce is a relatively mild hot sauce that tastes a little like spicy ketchup. Chili paste is a devilishly hot condiment made with pureed red chilies, vinegar, garlic, and salt. A Singaporean would use the Indonesian version: sambal ulek. You can also use Chinese chili garlic sauce or Vietnamese hot sauce. *Serves 4*

219 CALORIES PER SERVING; 15 G PROTEIN; 6 G FAT; 1 G SATURATED FAT; 28 G CARBOHYDRATE; 913 MG SODIUM; 29 MG CHOLESTEROL

# PAC-RIM
## PRIMAVERA

*Here's a Pac-Rim remake of an Italian-American classic, featuring a colorful assortment of Oriental vegetables.*
*There are many possibilities for noodles, including Western-style spaghetti or Chinese egg noodles.*
*(Use the fresh pre-steamed egg noodles sold in plastic bags in supermarket produce sections.)*

8 Chinese black mushrooms
8 ounces pre-steamed Chinese egg noodles
    (see Note on page 54) or spaghetti

FOR THE SAUCE:
½ cup Chicken Stock or Vegetable Stock
    (see pages 67–69)
¼ cup no-fat sour cream
3 tablespoons rice wine or dry sherry
3 tablespoons oyster sauce (see Note on
    page 32)
2 teaspoons cornstarch
½ to 1 teaspoon chili oil or hot sauce
salt and freshly ground black pepper

. . .

1 tablespoon canola oil
3 cloves garlic, minced
1 tablespoon minced fresh ginger
3 scallions, white part minced, green part
    thinly sliced on the diagonal
2 carrots, scrubbed and julienned
1 red bell pepper, cored, seeded, and julienned
2 cups thinly sliced nappa (Chinese cabbage)
2 cups snow peas (6 ounces), stems and
    strings removed
salt and freshly ground black pepper to taste
2 tablespoons black sesame seeds (optional)

1. Bring 4 quarts of water to a boil in a large pot for cooking the noodles. Soak the mushrooms in hot water to cover for 20 minutes, or until soft.

2. Stem the mushrooms and thinly slice. Cook the noodles until al dente: Egg noodles will take about 4 to 6 minutes, spaghetti about 8 minutes. Drain the noodles in a colander, rinse

with cold water, and drain again. Combine the ingredients for the sauce and whisk until the sour cream and cornstarch are dissolved.

3. Heat a large wok (preferably nonstick) over a high flame and swirl in the canola oil. Add the garlic, ginger, and scallion whites and stir-fry until fragrant but not brown, about 15 seconds. Add the carrots, pepper, cabbage, snow

peas, and mushrooms and stir-fry until crispy-tender, about 2 minutes. Stir the sauce to redissolve the cornstarch and add it to the vegetables. Bring the sauce to a boil. Stir in the noodles and stir-fry until thoroughly heated, about 2 minutes. Correct the seasoning, adding salt or pepper to taste. Sprinkle the noodles with the scallion greens and black sesame seeds, if using, and serve at once.

*Serves 4*

298 CALORIES PER SERVING; 11 G PROTEIN; 5 G FAT; 1 G SATURATED FAT; 50 G CARBOHYDRATE; 99 MG SODIUM; 42 MG CHOLESTEROL

# BASIC RECIPES

## CHICKEN STOCK

*Good stock is the prerequisite for good cooking. This is especially true for high-flavor, low-fat cooking. Stock can be substituted for cream in some pasta dishes and for butter or oil in others. It perfumes your house and gives you wonderfully moist cooked chicken, which you will need for several of the recipes in this book.*

*Some people are put off by the idea of making stock, but nothing could be easier. There are really only two things to remember. First, after the initial boiling, gently simmer the stock and don't let it boil again. (If you do, the fat will homogenize and the broth will become cloudy.) Second, skim the stock often with a shallow ladle. This removes any fat and impurities and it keeps the stock clean.*

*Homemade chicken stock tastes infinitely better than the canned variety and is dramatically lower in sodium. Here's a basic recipe. To make dark stock, use chicken parts (backs, wings, necks, etc.) and roast them and the vegetables in a roasting pan in a 400°F oven until very dark brown. A roasted turkey carcass makes a wonderful dark stock.*

3½- to 4-pound chicken

FOR THE SPICE BUNDLE:
4 large parsley sprigs or parsley stems
4 fresh thyme sprigs or 1 teaspoon dried thyme
2 bay leaves
10 peppercorns
2 allspice berries
2 cloves

· · ·

1 large onion, quartered
1 leek, trimmed, washed, and cut into 1-inch
   pieces (optional)
3 carrots, cut into 1-inch pieces
3 stalks celery, cut into 1-inch pieces
1 head of garlic, cut in half
4 quarts cold water, or as needed

*Western Pasta*

1. Remove any lumps of fat from the chicken. (For a leaner broth, remove the skin, too.) Wash the bird and drain. Make the spice bundle: tie the herbs, peppercorns, allspice berries, and cloves in a piece of cheesecloth or wrap them in a square of aluminum foil, which you pierce all over with a fork. (The latter is a high-tech bouquet garni.)

2. Place the chicken, spice bundle, and vegetables in a large pot and add cold water to cover by 2 inches. (You'll need about 4 quarts of water.) Bring the stock to a boil and skim off any foam that rises to the surface. Lower the heat and gently simmer until the chicken is cooked, about 1 hour. Add cold water as necessary to keep the chicken covered. Skim the stock often, especially after you've added water. (The cold water brings the fat to the top.)

3. Transfer the chicken to a bowl and let cool. When cool, pull the meat off the bones. (You can keep the shredded pieces of cooked chicken in a plastic container in your refrigerator to use in various recipes.) Return the bones to the stockpot. Continue simmering the stock until richly flavored and reduced to 10 to 12 cups, about 1 hour more.

4. Strain the stock into clean containers and let cool to room temperature. Stock will keep for 3 to 4 days in the refrigerator, for several months in the freezer.

**Note:** For an extra-clear stock, pour the stock through a strainer lined with cheesecloth or paper towels. This is how my wife, Barbara, makes stock, and hers is as clear as crystal.

*Makes 10 to 12 cups*

# VEGETABLE STOCK

*Here's a stock for our vegetarian friends. It's easier to make than chicken stock, because it requires almost no skimming. Almost any vegetable or vegetable trimming is a candidate for stock: tomato skins and seeds, corncobs and husks, summer and winter squash, red and yellow peppers, green beans, zucchini, mushrooms, potatoes, collard greens, and kale stalks. Use strong-tasting vegetables, such as green peppers, eggplants, turnips, and cabbage in moderation, since their flavor tends to be overpowering. Avoid beets, which will turn a stock red, and artichokes, which will make it bitter.*

1 large onion, skin on, quartered
2 leeks, trimmed, washed, and cut into 1-inch pieces
2 carrots, cut into 1-inch pieces
2 stalks celery, cut into 1-inch pieces
2 tomatoes, cut into 1-inch pieces
6 garlic cloves, skin on, cut in half
2 quarts chopped vegetables or vegetable trimmings (see above for suggested vegetables)

2 tablespoons tomato paste
2 bay leaves
½ cup mixed chopped fresh herbs, including basil, oregano, chives, and/or parsley stems (optional)
4 quarts water
freshly ground black pepper
sea salt or soy sauce to taste (optional)

1. Combine the ingredients in a stockpot and bring to a boil. Reduce the heat and simmer the stock, uncovered, for 1 to 1½ hours, or until well flavored, adding water as necessary to keep the vegetables covered. (A certain amount of evaporation will take place—this helps concentrate the flavor.) Skim the stock as necessary and season with pepper and salt or soy sauce to taste at the end. Alternatively, the stock can be cooked in a pressure cooker for 15 minutes.

2. Strain the stock, pressing with the back of a spoon to extract as much liquid as possible from the vegetables. Cool the stock to room temperature, then refrigerate or freeze. For a thicker, richer stock, force the liquid and vegetables through a vegetable mill or puree in a blender, then strain.

**Note:** I like to freeze 1-cup portions of vegetable stock, so I always have the right amount on hand. *Makes 2½ to 3½ quarts. (Yield will vary, depending on the vegetables used, the size of the pot, and the length of the cooking time.)*

# PASTA PRIMER: GUIDE TO SHAPES AND SIZES

Over the centuries, pasta makers have developed literally hundreds of different pasta shapes. The realm of Asian pasta is equally diverse. Here's a guide to some of the many pasta shapes found in a well-stocked market. (See photos on pages 66 and 70.)

**Note:** Unless otherwise stated, the following refer to dried pasta.

## WESTERN PASTA

*bucatini:* a long, hollow noodle that looks like fat spaghetti.

*capellini:* "little hairs," super-thin egg noodles. Sometimes called *capelli d'angelo,* literally "angel hair."

*cavatappi:* "corkscrews," twisted, ridged macaroni.

*cavatelli:* a dried pasta from the south of Italy that resembles an elongated cowrie shell.

*conchiglie:* "conchshells," oval pasta shells. Small shells are called *conchigliette.*

*couscous:* tiny pelletlike noodles made by forcing pasta dough through a sieve. Couscous is a mainstay of the North African diet. It is one of the few pastas that are served completely cooked, not al dente.

*ditali:* stubby, ridged pasta tubes.

*farfalle:* "butterflies," pasta bows.

*fedelini:* thin spaghetti.

*fettuccine:* flat ¼-inch-wide egg noodles (originally from Rome).

*fusilli:* "springs," pasta coiled like a corkscrew. Fusilli can range in length from 3 to 10 inches.

*gemelli:* "twins," short pasta twists. A similar pasta bears the colorful name *strozzapreti,* "priest strangler."

*gnocchi:* a small ridged pasta shell that resembles a similarly named Italian potato dumpling.

*lasagne:* broad, ribbonlike noodles often with rippled edges.

*Asian Pasta*

*linguine:* flat spaghetti.

*macaroni:* small, elbow-shaped tubes immortalized by Yankee Doodle. Tiny ones are called *maccheroncini.*

*orecchiette:* "little ears," small, cupped, disk-shaped pasta from the south of Italy.

*orzo:* a tiny pasta shaped like a grain of rice. Small orzo are called *risoni.*

*pappardelle:* wide (½ to 1 inch) ribbons of egg noodle.

*penne:* "quills," pasta tubes with ends cut on the diagonal. *Penette* are tiny penne.

*perciatelli:* another long, hollow noodle that looks like fat spaghetti. (A little smaller than bucatini.)

*raditori:* "radiators," convoluted radiator-shaped pasta twists.

*rigati:* ridged pasta tubes. (More generally speaking, the term refers to any pasta with a ridged surface.)

*rigatoni:* large, ridged, curved pasta tubes.

*rotelle:* coiled pasta twists. *Rotini* are small twists.

*ruote di carro:* "cartwheels," round pasta wheels with spokes and a hub in the center. *Note:* Some companies call these *rotelle.*

*spaghetti:* a long, stringlike noodle that's one of the world's most popular pastas. Skinny spaghetti is called *spaghettini.*

*tagliatelle:* the classic flat egg noodle of Bologna. *Tagliatelle* are slightly wider than fettuccine. *Tagliolini* are similar, but much narrower.

*taglierini:* thin, narrow ribbons of egg pasta.

*tonnarelli:* square spaghetti made of egg pasta.

*tubetti:* small, short pasta tubes used for soup.

*vermicelli:* "little worms," very thin noodles.

*ziti:* short, squat tubes similar to rigatoni, but with smooth walls.

## ASIAN NOODLES

Noodles are widely popular throughout Asia—as much as if not more so than in Italy! Their internationalism gives rise to an almost Babylonian confusion with nomenclature. Wheat noodles, for example, are called *mian* in Mandarin, *mein* in Cantonese, *somen* in Japanese, *mee* in Thai, and *gougsou* in Korean. The Oriental penchant for giving foods picturesque names (such as "cellophane" or "shining" noodles) adds to the confusion. Here's a guide to the major players.

*Note:* The internationalization of the American diet has made Asian noodles increasingly available. Most of the items can be found at gourmet shops, natural foods stores, and even supermarkets. (Dried noodles will be in the ethnic foods section, fresh and pre-steamed noodles in the produce section.)

*bean threads* (also known as cellophane noodles, shining noodles, glass noodles, vermicelli, and by the Chinese name *fan si,* "powdered silk"): thin, translucent noodles made from mung bean starch. Bean threads have a chewy, slightly gelatinous texture much prized by the Chinese. Soak them in cold water to soften, then cook in boiling water for a minute or two. Bean threads are often sold in small packages in net bags.

*dumpling wrapper* (also known as gyoza skins): paper-thin circles of fresh wheat noodle dough used for making dumplings. (*Gyoza* is the Japanese word for dumpling.) Look for dumpling wrappers in the produce section of many supermarkets and at Asian markets, where they're sold both fresh and frozen. I like to think of dumpling wrappers as ready-made pasta dough—ideal for making Western-style ravioli. One good brand is Frieda's.

*egg noodles:* yellowish Chinese wheat noodles made with flour and eggs. Asian markets carry fresh egg noodles. Most supermarkets carry pre-steamed egg noodles, which are partially cooked and conveniently packaged in sealed plastic bags. One widely available brand is Leasa.

*ramen:* wheat noodles usually sold dried in tightly coiled blocks, often in single-serving portions. Ramen is the Japanese name. *Gan mian* is the Chinese name for a similar noodle.

*rice sticks/rice noodles:* This covers a large family of noodles made from rice flour and water

that are popular throughout Southeast Asia. Rice noodles can be as thin as angel hair or as wide as fettuccine. Soak in cold water for 20 minutes to soften, then cook in boiling water for 1 to 3 minutes. *Note:* Rice noodles absorb broth like crazy, so it's important to serve the dish as soon as it's cooked.

*soba:* a slender gray-brown buckwheat noodle from Japan. Often enjoyed chilled. *Cha soba* ("tea noodle") is a buckwheat noodle flavored and colored with green tea. Koreans have a similar noodle, called *naeng myun.*

*somen:* a very slender, delicate, white wheat noodle from Japan. *Shiso somen* are wheat noodles flavored with pickled plum and beefsteak leaf.

*udon:* a thick, chewy wheat noodle from Japan. Some udon are square, others round; most are white. Most natural foods stores and gourmet shops sell dried udon; if you live near an Asian market, you may be able to find fresh or frozen fresh udon.

*wonton wrappers:* paper-thin squares of fresh wheat noodle dough used for making wontons and other dumplings. Look for wonton wrappers in the produce section of many supermarkets and at Asian markets, where they're sold both fresh and frozen. One widely available brand is Leasa. Wonton wrappers are ideal for making Western-style ravioli.

# INDEX

*Page numbers in italics refer to illustrations.*